Face to Face
With God
Biblical Meditation

Mintie Nel & Jan Whitmore

Scripture quoted from the Holy Bible:

The New King James Version, Copyright 1979, 1980, 1982 by Thomas Nelson. Used with permission.

New International Version, Copyright 1973, 1978, 1984 by International Bible Society Used with permission from Hodder & Stoughton.

The Message. Copyright © 1993, 1994, 1995, 1996, 2000, 2001, 2002. Used by permission of NavPress Publishing Group

The Amplified® Bible, Copyright © 1954, 1958, 1962, 1964, 1965, 1987 by The Lockman Foundation Used by permission. (www.Lockman.org)

Book cover artist: SelfPubBookCovers.com/FrinaArt

Internal design: Jan Whitmore

Certain stock imagery: Dreamstime LLC; Thinkstock

Anyone depicted in stock imagery provided by Dreamstime and Thinkstock are models and such images are being used for illustrative purposes only.

DEDICATION

We dedicate this book to cross-cultural Christian missionaries serving all over the world. Thank you for your obedience, your faithfulness and deep devotion to the call of God. Thank you for laying down your lives for others. Thank you for bringing healing and reconciliation to the world through the Gospel of Jesus Christ. Thank you for the sacrifices you have made. Finish well!

We count it an honour to serve you.

Mintie Nel and Jan Whitmore

Face to Face with God

CONTENTS

Face to Face with God

ACKNOWLEDGEMENTS

This book represents a lifetime of learning about the power of God's Word and applying its eternal truth. Biblical meditation has transformed our lives and ministry. We truly believe that Biblical meditation lies at the heart of being a fruitful disciple of Jesus.

While writing this book we have seen the beauty of the Body of Christ working together. We are grateful to God for those who came alongside to see this project through. We have needed the support of friends, encouragers, intercessors, editors and proofreaders. We particularly thank the Lord for the skills of each of the following: Maritha Esterhuizen (editing), Jeanne Cilliers (editing), Gweno Hugh-Jones (editing and proof reading), Mary Atkins (proof reading), Reuven and Yanit Ross (encouragement and contributors). We would have given up if it were not for the demonstration of their devotion to the task and us.

We have had the privilege of coming alongside and helping many cross-cultural missionaries. In the book we have shared stories which we feel will help others. To protect identities we have changed names and invented new locations. Events and scenarios may sound familiar but that should not be surprising; they are common to many believers.

FOREWORD

We are thrilled that Mintie and Jan have written this excellent book on Biblical meditation! We have felt for a long time that the Body of Christ has desperately needed this teaching, and knew of none more qualified to write material on this subject. They have studied this topic extensively, live it daily and have taught it to numerous groups of believers over the years. This teaching is not just the fruit of their studies, but of their own lives. It is incarnate in them.

We met Mintie Nel and Jan Whitmore in Jerusalem, Israel, in the 1980's. Little did we know at that time that our lives would be linked together for many years to come, with blessing upon blessing! Mintie and Jan have become dear friends of ours. They are both very creative and talented, deeply spiritual and delightfully humorous. They are passionate in their love for God and His Word. Over the last two decades, we have spent holidays, shared many meals and prayer times, laughed and cried together. We have worked alongside one another in ministry on a few continents. As we have seen them live what they teach and preach, we can enthusiastically recommend this book as well as any of their other materials.

When we first sat under their teaching on Biblical meditation at a retreat for missionaries, we were amazed that we had somehow missed the importance of this significant spiritual discipline. We had read the Word daily for years, studied it regularly and taught it, yet we had failed to *meditate* on it as they suggested we do. We were convicted and convinced by the Word of God, their testimonies and their devotional lives.

Biblical meditation is a lost art for most modern believers, and yet it is the discipline that shapes our thought processes and influences our words and behaviour more than any other. The enemy fights hard to keep us too busy and distracted to take the time necessary to quietly sit in the Lord's presence and meditate on His Word. Our tendency to be over-committed and vigorously active prevents us from dwelling deeply with God. In these days, the Holy Spirit is impressing upon many of us in the Church to live more simply and prioritise our commitments so that we can spend more time in His presence.

With the many promises in the Word of God related to Biblical meditation, we should make this discipline a daily part of our devotional lives. Abiding in His Word yields incredible results for this life and the next. What you are about to read has power to revolutionise your life – *if* you will walk in it. We pray that you will receive the *full* impact of the truths conveyed in this book.

Reuven and Yanit Ross

Making Disciples International

www.making-disciples.net

Mintie Nel & Jan Whitmore

PREFACE

Years ago, when I (Mintie Nel) first learned how to hear the voice of the Lord I had a remarkable experience. God gave me a very specific message. Little did I realise that this message would take me on a physical and spiritual journey, which would span a lifetime. I was 22 years old.

I had trained as a social worker and completed my first year of practical social work in 1972. I sensed that God was speaking to me about fulltime Christian work. Was this a calling to go to the mission field? It was while I was being discipled by Rea Uys, a wonderful godly woman, that I was advised to wait on the Lord for a specific passage of Scripture, which would give me guidance and direction. It sounded like an exciting adventure and I was eager to hear from the Lord!

One day I opened my Bible at Ezekiel 2: 1-5, a passage of Scripture I was not familiar with. The words seemed to leap from the page. Instead of reading Ezekiel's call, I heard the Lord say, "Mintie, you stand up on your feet and I will speak to you. I am sending you to the Israelites, to a rebellious nation, which has rebelled against me; they and their ancestors have been in revolt against me to this very day. The people to whom I am sending you are obstinate and stubborn. Say to them, 'This is what the Sovereign LORD says.' And whether they listen or fail to listen—for they are a rebellious house—they will know that a prophet has been among them".

I was overwhelmed and I kept repeating these words over and over in my mind. I questioned the Lord daily, "Does this mean I have to leave South Africa and go to the land of Israel? Can't I work amongst the Jews here in South Africa?" Then He spoke to me again, "Get out of your country, from your family and from your father's house, to a land which I will show you" (Genesis 12: 1 NKJV).

For days, I felt God's Word burning within my heart and I started to believe and understand that this was exactly what God wanted me to do. Without any doubt, I knew God was calling and sending me to go to the land of Israel. God was speaking to me personally and this was what I had to do. I received these specific words directly from God, written down more than 2,500 years ago in the book of Ezekiel. How amazing that in 1972 I heard and received the very same message from the Lord. God was calling me to fulltime service, a calling I have been following for over 40 years.

Eat the Word

However, this was not the end of the message. God had definitely given me a geographical call, but what would I do there? In the same passage, God went on to say, "Open your mouth, *and eat* what I am giving you" (Ezekiel 2: 8, NKJV, emphasis added). Then Ezekiel saw a hand holding a book, which contained God's words for His people. He opened his mouth and *ate* the book. It tasted sweet like honey. It was then that God said to Ezekiel, "Go… and speak my words unto them" (Ezekiel 3: 4 NKJV).

I pondered these words. Why did He say it in such a way? First Ezekiel was to eat and then he would speak what he had eaten! God was speaking a clear word that would prepare me for ministry, "Eat My words and let these words become part of you. Then go and speak to others the words you have eaten." What an important principle to learn! You cannot pass on what you have not experienced or do not know as truth in your heart. The only words worth giving to the people of Israel would be the words I had eaten and digested from God's precious Word, the Holy Bible.

This revelation had a profound impact on my young life and since then I have become a disciple of God and a student of the Word, making it my very own.

His Thoughts Became Mine

Biblical meditation became the digestive system of my soul and spirit. I started to understand and experience God's character, His ways, His nature and His desires by what I ate and ingested. The Word of God became an integral part, renewing and transforming my heart and mind, and in doing so, it provided the means of fulfilling the call of God for the rest of my life. The Holy Spirit established God's Word in my mind and wrote it on the flesh of my heart (Jeremiah 31: 33 NKJV). With God's instruction and guidance within me, I became confident in the knowledge that I am able to both think and do according to His will. My thoughts and desires started coming into line with His thoughts and desires (Psalm 37: 4).

Even Jesus followed this divine pattern as He lived under His Father's authority here on earth. Jesus said, "… I do nothing of Myself; *but as My Father taught Me, I speak these things.* And He who sent Me is with Me. The Father has not left Me alone, for I always do those things which please Him" (John 8: 28-29 NKJV, emphasis added). John also records Jesus as saying, "I speak what I have seen *with* My Father" (John 8: 38 NKJV, emphasis added). "*With*", meaning close to, near to, in the Father's presence, places the focus on being close to (having relationship with) the Father in order to know His thoughts and desires and do His will.

"That which was from the beginning, which *we have* heard, which *we have* seen with our eyes, which *we have* looked upon, and *our hands* have handled, concerning the Word of life—the life was manifested, and *we have* seen, and bear witness, and declare to you that eternal life which was with the Father and was manifested to us—*that which we have seen and heard we declare to you*, that you also may have fellowship with us; and truly our fellowship is with the Father and with His Son Jesus Christ. And these things we write to you that your joy may be full." (1 John 1: 1-4 NKJV, emphasis added).

I made this my motto for life: I speak what I know and have found to be true in Christ Jesus! I pray that this book, formed over a lifetime, will offer teaching and direction. It is a study to be experienced. You too will discover the power of God hidden in the pages of the Bible. This is the pathway to a deeper and closer walk with Jesus.

In 1973 while in Israel, I contracted scarlet fever and rheumatic fever simultaneously, which resulted in rheumatoid arthritis (RA) in all my joints. RA is a chronic illness, which causes a high degree of pain and discomfort most of the time. Thankfully, with help, it has not deterred me from fulfilling the call of God on my life! I can honestly say that Biblical meditation has kept me strong in the Lord, focused on His strength and His enabling. I am very grateful to God that I found His secret diet for a healthy spiritual life in spite of the daily physical challenges of severe pain and discomfort caused by my swollen joints. Biblical meditation produces joy in the Lord and that gives me strength to endure, persevere and overcome daily.

I left Israel in 1991 to join Jan Whitmore (née Jan Rowland) in founding a new international itinerant ministry of encouragement to missionaries—Mission Encouragement Trust, a UK charity. I am so thankful for the contribution of Jan to the writing of this discipleship book. My friend, carer and colleague has kindly taken my notes, added some of her own insights and understanding and assembled this significant teaching on Biblical meditation.

She is the author of *Sow What*, the first book of a discipleship series, to which *Face to Face with God* has now been added. Inspired by the parable of the sower it presents a depth of unique revelation and insight about spiritual growth. It is transformational.

Studying *Sow What?* will prepare you for *Face to Face with God* but equally *Face to Face with God* will lay an excellent foundation for *Sow What?* They make excellent back-to-back studies! Doubtless, more discipleship books will be coming soon.

www.makingdisciples.co.uk

Mintie Nel & Jan Whitmore

9

CHAPTER ONE

An Introduction to the Study

"Biblical meditation is perhaps the most neglected of all devotional practices in the Church, yet it is also one of the most profitable."
—Campbell McAlpine

This is a journey into abundant life through Biblical meditation. The content of this book, if applied, has the potential to renew your life from the inside out. For years you may have skimmed the surface of the Bible, but in the coming weeks you will be encouraged to let the Holy Spirit embed God's Word deeply into your heart, for the purpose of spiritual transformation. The Apostle Paul says:

> "Let the word of Christ dwell in you richly in all wisdom, teaching and admonishing one another in psalms and hymns and spiritual songs, singing with grace in your hearts to the Lord. And whatever you do in word or deed, do all in the name of the Lord Jesus, giving thanks to God the Father through Him" (Colossians 3: 16-17 NKJV).

The book is not a theoretical explanation of what Biblical meditation is to gain head-knowledge. We want you *to experience* the goodness of the Word of God through instruction, practice and application. Truth is not readily exposed or grasped by quick or random "Bible-dipping"; hidden treasure must be searched for by digging deeply (Luke 6: 48) and this requires both devotion and time.

We share insights gained at the coalface of ministry. Many times when ministering to missionaries, we encountered difficult and complex circumstances for which we had little or no wisdom. Aided by the Holy Spirit, we needed to find answers in God's Word. Few believers would doubt that God's Word is a lamp to our feet and a light to our path—the Bible tells us so (Psalm 119: 105)—but to experience the reality of that truth in specific situations and circumstances establishes deeper faith. Scripture is to become reality *in us,* leading us to full assurance of its truth.

When we pause to seek the Lord and meditate upon specific passages of Scripture, the entrance of truth increases our knowledge and experience of God's character and ways, firing up a living faith within. We become authentic—internal transformation influences and shapes attitudes and conduct. Psalm 119: 130 describes it this way:

> "The entrance of Your words gives light; it gives understanding to the simple" (NKJV).

Getting the Best out of this Discipleship Study

This book is rewarding as a personal or group devotional study. However, forming a "life group" is often more advantageous. After studying each chapter alone, we recommend meeting weekly with a few fellow disciples of Jesus to discuss the questions, which the study offers for consideration. It gives opportunity to build relationships and learn from one another. The rich benefits derived from disciplined Biblical meditation will bring you much closer to the Lord, each other and accelerate spiritual development.

At the back of the book, you will find Appendix 1: "Forming a Life Group" which gives clear guidelines for such a group. During a preliminary meeting, the group can read this appendix together. Agreement on the structure, purpose and function of the group will establish a strong foundation upon which trust can grow, and this will open up the way towards real, honest and open sharing during the following weeks.

The first five chapters of *Face to Face with God* provide a foundational understanding of Biblical meditation. Chapters 6 to 9 will help you practice integrating and applying what you are learning. In addition, at the back of the book you will find Appendix 2—A Guide to Meditating upon the Word of God and Appendix 3—Seven Bible Meditations to Strengthen Faith.

Preparing Yourself

This study should be a focused period of intentional listening to the Lord, with a willingness to learn from Him. Resist any proud attitude which says, "I already know this!" Even if you have learned some of these aspects in the past, let your heart learn them again. The Holy Spirit brings fresh revelation to the one who is humble of heart— even on subjects studied during bygone years. Many of us "know the Scriptures" in our heads, we can even quote them verbatim, but few have allowed the Scriptures to transform their lives to the point where they can give examples or testimony of how God's Word has worked in the grit of life.

The following steps are very important to take before the start of each chapter:

- Prayerfully consecrate yourself …
    o Kneel, bow your head, lay flat on your face, lift your hands—*do* something. Let your actions mirror your heart.
- Consciously yield your body, soul (mind, will and emotions) and spirit to the Lord.
- Ask the Holy Spirit to teach, lead and guide you through this study.

- Diarise study times. Make this time of discipleship a sacred appointment with God—a priority. Switch off and remove all distractions.

We are Disciples of Jesus

To understand the significance of Biblical meditation in discipleship we need to reflect on the rabbi / disciple relationship of Jesus' day.

A rabbi was a person who distinguished himself by his passion to study, teach, interpret and live the Torah. It was custom for rabbis to take a group of disciples under their own tutelage. They were often ordinary lay-folk—blacksmiths, tailors, farmers, fishermen, tanners, shoemakers, woodcutters, and carpenters who were not paid. They relied on the hospitality of hosts. It was natural, therefore, for disciples to adopt the same lifestyle. Their daily routine and discipline included poring over the sacred scrolls "day and night" and travelling with the rabbi village to village as he taught in the synagogues. Disciples would observe, listen and copy his ways. As disciples learned, so their rabbi would send them out on their own.

In like manner, Jesus chose His disciples and they followed Him from place to place, observing His character and teaching methods. Listening carefully to His interpretation of the Scriptures, they rubbed shoulders, interacting and asking questions about His words and His actions. It would be true to say that they not only meditated upon the Word of God but on the person of Jesus. In the context of relationship, they became like Him. It is instructive to think that when Jesus left this earth to return to the Father, the life-giving message preached to the world was fuelled by their meditation of Him. This, too, is our model for discipleship. John says it this way:

"That which was from the beginning, which we have heard, which we have seen with our eyes, which we have looked upon, and our hands have handled, concerning the Word of life—the life was manifested, and we have seen, and bear witness, and declare to you that eternal life which was with the Father and was manifested to us—that which we have seen and heard we declare to you, that you also may have fellowship with us; and truly our fellowship is with the Father and with His Son Jesus Christ. And these things we write to you that your joy may be full" (1 John 1: 1-4 NKJV).

The Nature of the Word

The Bible is an extraordinary book; every word, precept, statute, description and account is God-inspired, God-breathed. Chosen scribes penned the words of God. As instructed by our heavenly Father, the Holy Spirit still takes, what appears to the natural mind to be dry words on a page, and gives them life as we apply them to our hearts and act upon them in everyday living. Inner transformation takes place as the Living Word, Jesus, teaches, rebukes, corrects and trains our hearts in righteousness, resulting in effective service! The Apostle Paul says:

"All Scripture is God-breathed and is useful for teaching, rebuking, correcting and training in righteousness, so that the man of God may be thoroughly equipped for every good work".

2 Timothy 3: 16-17 NIV

When we ingest the God-breathed Word, we literally take the life of God into our inner life—our body, soul (mind, will and emotions) and spirit. The Bible says that God intends to renew our carnal minds and transform our lives. How? By means of Biblical meditation, we absorb the Word of God to the point of integration where it becomes the only plumb-line of our character, conduct and choices.

Biblical meditation is God's prescribed means for bringing His life-changing Word into our heart. Every disciple of Jesus can hear the voice of the Lord by spending protracted time meditating on the Holy Scriptures. This is still the most common way God speaks today. There are other ways of hearing His voice, for example through prophecy, visions and words of knowledge but they must be tested against the written Word. God will never speak contrary to His written Word. Be wary of listening to "the word of the Lord" from someone who is not meditating on the God-breathed Word day and night. Their words may be of the flesh rather than of the Spirit.

Do you realise that we meditate all the time – either consciously or subconsciously? It is so, no matter what our age. Apparently we have ten thousand thoughts a day which lead to desire and then to action. Minute by minute we are thinking about something and every action owes its existence to one of those thoughts. Here are some examples:

- An image catches our eye and we think about it. Lengthy meditation on the image arouses desire, and desire leads to action. This may be positive or negative.
- Something worries us and fills our mind with anxious thoughts which we tend to rehearse. The thoughts disturb our hearts—we experience various emotions. This rehearsal of thought is meditation.
- When a person upsets us, we tend to examine and re-examine the event. Our mind and heart eagerly agree on what should happen next. Examination and re-examination is meditation.
- Occasionally we are paid a compliment and we savour those words, pondering them. Pondering is meditation.

All these actions are meditation. What we see, hear and experience shapes beliefs, values and the direction of our lives.

The Challenge of this Study

The challenge of this study is not to convince readers that they *should* or even *must* meditate; the challenge of this book is to encourage participants to realise that *the focus* of their meditation is of utmost importance. For our benefit, God commands that He remains our meditation. When we really love Him, He will consume our thoughts. Simply put, meditation upon God's Word is meditating upon Him— His character, His nature, His ways, His glory, His Kingdom. He is our salvation, sanctification, life, health and well-being. To love God with heart, soul, mind and strength is the perfect definition of Biblical meditation.

Jesus said:

> "The first of all the commandments is: 'Hear, O Israel, the LORD our God, the LORD is one. And you shall love the LORD your God with all your heart, with all your soul, with all your mind, and with all your strength.' This is the first commandment. And the second, like it, is this: 'You shall love your neighbour as yourself.' There is no other commandment greater than these" (Mark 12: 29-31 NKJV).

Biblical meditation will always be offensive to selfishness; our flesh will moan and strongly resist any sort of discipline and call to change. Whilst selfish thought is as natural as life, concentrating on God is not—it requires disciplined obedience. Our default focus is self, the world and sin. None need teaching and training on how to meditate on those things! Biblical meditation switches the focus from self-preoccupation to God-preoccupation and that, in time, leads to spiritual maturity and fruitfulness.

Two Things of Which to be Aware:

1. Spiritual attack. Biblical meditation provokes Satan and his spirit agents.
2. Confusion. Not all meditation is of God.

1. Spiritual Attack

We recommend that for the duration of the study the Life Group becomes the means of extra support and strength in prayer. Cover each other's backs. Satan targets Christians who are being transformed into the likeness of Jesus and who are becoming victorious overcomers.

The Apostle Peter gives us the following instructions:

> "Be sober; be vigilant; because your adversary the devil walks about like a roaring lion, seeking whom he may devour. Resist him, steadfast in the faith, knowing that the same sufferings are experienced by your brotherhood in the world" (1 Peter 5: 8-10 NKJV).

There may be subtle attacks on your personal life or on the lives of those dear to you. The Apostle Paul alludes to these by mentioning marriage, parents, children, housekeepers and bosses at work before he says:

> "Finally, my brethren, be strong in the Lord and in the power of His might. Put on the whole armour of God, so that you may be able to stand against the wiles of the devil. For we do not wrestle against flesh and blood, but against principalities, against powers, against the rulers of the darkness of this age, against

spiritual hosts of wickedness in the heavenly places. Therefore, take up the whole armour of God, so that you may be able to withstand in the evil day, and having done all, to stand. Stand therefore ..." (Ephesians 6: 10-14 NKJV).

Remember to put on your spiritual armour. God supplies spiritual armour and weapons; never go to war unarmed, because you will be killed, robbed and destroyed - Ephesians 6: 10-17; John 10: 10a.

Put on the:
- a. Belt of truth
- b. Breastplate of righteousness
- c. Battle shoes of readiness
- d. Shield of faith
- e. Helmet of salvation
- f. Sword of the Spirit

Know that:
- a. God in us gives us the victory - 1 John 4: 4
- b. We overcome by the blood of Jesus and the word of our testimony - Revelation 12: 11

2. Don't get Confused

Biblical meditation is distinct from all other forms of meditation. Not all meditation is born of the Holy Spirit!

- **Biblical meditation is <u>not</u>** the emptying of our minds so as to think about nothing.
  - o It is *not* staring into space, getting into a "zone" or practising Eastern/transcendental meditation—these are not of the Holy Spirit. The danger of "emptying" your mind and remaining in some trance-like state is that Satan

and his demons may use the opportunity to invade and occupy. Read Luke 11: 24-26.

- **Biblical meditation is <u>not</u>** the act of taking time to dream and think about ourselves.
  - o It is not meditating to become positive or assertive.
  - o The object of Biblical meditation is a Person—the God of Abraham, Isaac and Jacob—our heavenly Father, His Son Jesus and the Holy Spirit.

- **Biblical meditation is <u>not</u>** a walk in nature to meditate on self in relationship to our surroundings.
  - o That is meditation born of self; it is not of the Holy Spirit.

- **Biblical meditation is <u>not</u>** an optional extra or an extracurricular activity for believers in Jesus Christ.
  - o God commanded Joshua to speak God's Word, meditate on it, and observe it—day and night (Joshua 1: 8). It is a discipline to which all believers are called to engage day and night; it is a mandatory part of serving and worshipping God. Read 1 Corinthians 9: 24-27. The Apostle Paul regards discipline as absolutely necessary to keep on track.

Prayer

Loving Father, thank You for every opportunity You bring for spiritual growth. Thank you for this study and I ask You to speak to me through it. Teach me how to meditate upon Your character, nature, principles, thoughts, ways and feelings, as revealed in the Bible. I want to lay aside all else to know You. Amen.

Questions to Consider and Answer

1. What do you anticipate during this season of study? Write down at least three expectations.
2. What is *your* definition of Biblical meditation? Write a few sentences in your own words.

Life Group

1. Introduce yourself. Briefly share where and when you received Jesus into your life.
2. Describe what you believe about the Word of God (The Bible). How did you become convinced of that?
3. Share your answers to the questions you considered at home.
4. Have one person pray for the group as it embarks on this season of study.

Scripture for Meditation

"For this reason I bow my knees to the Father of our Lord Jesus Christ, from whom the whole family in heaven and earth is named, that He would grant you, according to the riches of His glory, to be strengthened with might through His Spirit in the inner man, that Christ may dwell in your hearts through faith; that you, being rooted and grounded in love, may be able to comprehend with all the saints what is the width and length and depth and height—to know the love of Christ which passes knowledge; that you may be filled with all the fullness of God" (Ephesians 3: 14-19 NKJV).

CHAPTER TWO

What is Biblical Meditation?

"Holding the Word of God in your heart until it has
affected every phase of your life...this is meditation."
—Andrew Murray

Consider the following questions:

- How did Joshua know *how* to lead the children of Israel in
  social, spiritual and judicial matters?
- How did David know *what* the righteous thing was to do
  when Saul pursued him? How did he know *how* to rule Israel
  as King and *when* to go into battle and *when* not to?
- *From whom* did Solomon receive his wisdom to judge justly
  and later write Proverbs?
- *From whom* did Mary acquire the strength and endurance to
  watch her son die so brutally, and yet not lose hope?
- *How* did the Apostles know how to correctly interpret the
  Scriptures and write the New Testament, to teach not only
  their generation of new believers, but also the generations of
  believers to follow?

The answer to all these questions is that each person
meditated upon God, His acts and judgments and His divine Law—
His teaching and instruction. They pondered, contemplated, centred

their thoughts, considered, mused, and reflected with deep devotion.

God dwelt among His people, Israel. Whether encamped or on the move, God's presence was at the centre. Marked as His own, life revolved around honouring and pleasing Him. They were wholly dependent on His covenant love, provision, counsel and wisdom.

All the great men of God like Abraham, Isaac, Jacob, Joseph, Moses, Joshua, David, Matthew, Mark, Luke, Peter, John, James and Paul, intently and intentionally meditated upon God, His actions and His eternal Law (Torah) because God was their source of life. They did not always meditate upon a written word, but they did have a culture of meditation whereby they thought, spoke of and celebrated the accounts of God's intervention in history, passing down remembrances from generation to generation. Here are some examples of their meditation:

- The Creator of the sea, sky, earth, stars, sun, moon, animals and man.
- God's holiness whereby He judged sin in the Flood.
- God's mercy whereby He saved Noah and his family. Instructing Noah to build an ark before the Flood came expressed His great mercy and salvation for humankind.

- God's loving-kindness whereby He called Abraham and made a covenant with him which would shape redemption for Jew and Gentile.

- The eternal "I Am" (Exodus 3: 13-15). God is the living God, ever-present and all-sufficient. He spoke to Moses out of a burning bush, delivered Israel from Egypt, parted the Red Sea, produced water from a rock, poured manna from heaven, and led Israel through the wilderness by means of a pillar of fire by night and a cloud by day.

- God dwelling among them. At Mount Sinai the Israelites entered into God's covenant of love (Exodus 19: 5-8). The tabernacle of Moses was built according to the heavenly pattern and God came down and dwelt among them in the sanctuary. He would love, protect, and provide for Israel, His betrothed.

- God's faithfulness. He commanded that they celebrate His feasts annually to remember His goodness and faithfulness.

- God keeping His promises. He led Joshua and the children of Israel into Canaan, the Promised Land. By His power they destroyed the cities and strongholds of the heathen nations, taking possession of what was promised (Deuteronomy 11:24).

- God raising up David, a man after His own heart, as king of Israel. A shepherd boy became the shepherd His people, Israel. They would meditate on David's victories as well as the devastating consequences of sin after he had committed adultery with Bathsheba.

- God's choices of locations for significant events. For example, the temple being built on Mount Moriah, the place where Abraham had offered Isaac to God. Later it would be the Mount on which our heavenly Father offered His Son Jesus.

- God's voice through the prophets. He raised up prophets to rebuke and warn Israel about her apostasy and spiritual adultery.
- God keeping covenant in timely fashion. He never stopped loving His people Israel. After she had spent her allotted time in exile, God remembered His covenant and returned Judah to the Promised Land.

Meditation on God, His words and actions not only expressed deep love for God, but also awakened and cultivated faith in His promises. As we turn the pages into the New Testament, God continues to reveal Himself and His redemptive plan through Jesus, His Son, who is the image of His Father (Hebrews 1: 3).

The person of Jesus, His life, His message and His redemptive mission are now central to our meditation. In addition to the revelation of God in the Old Testament, we meditate upon the character and nature of Jesus, the cross, the resurrection, the coming of the Holy Spirit, the Kingdom of God and God's mandate to go and make disciples.

An eternal pattern is set:

"You shall love the LORD your God with all your heart, with all your soul, and with all your strength. And these words which I command you today shall be in your heart. You shall teach them diligently to your children, and shall talk of them when you sit in your house, when you walk by the way, when you lie down, and when you rise up. You shall bind them as a sign on your hand, and they shall be as frontlets between your eyes. You shall write them on the doorposts of your house and on your gates" (Deuteronomy 6: 5-9 NKJV).

Two Hebrew Words for Meditation

Two Hebrew words, *SIYACH* and *HAGAH* have been translated as *meditate* in the Bible. The English word "meditate" does not reflect the deep and rich meaning of the Hebrew equivalents.

Siyach

Siyach means to engage in contemplation or reflection, to focus one's thoughts on; reflect or ponder over; to plan or project in the mind, or to think about.

Siyach also means to cultivate, to converse, to reflect with deep devotion, to recite, to pray, to declare with quiet contemplation, to sing.

In Genesis 2: 5, the word *siyach* (noun) refers to the shoot of a plant in creation. *Siyach* (verb) means the action of *calling forth* the potential of the plant. Taking the two ideas together, God plants a seed from His Word, which grows to a shoot, and the Holy Spirit calls it forth into life.

Biblical meditation releases God's thoughts and feelings about every subject we meditate upon, bringing before us the choice of lining up our own mind and will with His. That which is pondered, reflected upon, considered, watered and nurtured to life becomes a rich inner storehouse. Paul says, "let the word of Christ dwell in you richly" (Colossians 3: 16).

We gain a richer, deeper and fuller understanding when we enter into the process of "Siyach-ing" (meditation), exploring and discovering the weight, depth and meaning of each word of a verse or passage. It is as if that which we think upon, expands and opens up within us, releasing the potential of the implanted shoot. Therefore, when we have meditated on a verse or passage of Scripture to the point of renewal of mind and change of heart, the next step is to declare it out loud—to release it. Praying the verse of Scripture, confessing it to God, and declaring it to others as a testimony, will cement its meaning and value in our heart. The Scriptures will burst to life within. With this regular and disciplined exercise, the very nature of Jesus, the living Word will come forth from our heart.

Here are a few Scriptures in which the word *siyach* is used.

1. The meaning of "*siyach*" has a vocal component.

   "Hear my voice, O God, hear my voice in my meditation (*siyach*)" (Psalm 64: 1 NKJV).

2. *Siyach's* primary focus is the splendour of God's majesty.

   "I will meditate (*siyach*) on the glorious splendour of Your majesty, and on Your wondrous works" (Psalm 145: 5 NKJV).

3. The night is a silent and quiet time during which one can see and hear what can't be heard and seen amidst the noise and distractions of the day.

   "My eyes are awake through the night watches, that I may meditate (*siyach*) on Your word" (Psalm 119: 148 NKJV).

4. Everything depends on what we see.

   "I will meditate (*siyach*) on Your precepts and contemplate Your ways" (Psalm 119: 15 NKJV).

Hagah

As in ancient Hebrew meditation, Scripture speaks when recited in a low murmur. This is murmuring to oneself—letting your own ears hear what you are saying. It is also murmuring before God so that He also hears the confession of your mouth.

> *Hagah* is the *process* of thinking—planning or projecting. It implies a careful weighing of a problem, reflecting on all parts of the issue. However, it does not necessarily mean that the flow of thought will draw us to a conclusion.

> *Hagah* also means to call to mind or to remember, to centre our thoughts on, or to form a mental picture of something or someone.

> *Hagah* means, "to utter in a low sound". It implies spoken worship, murmuring with pleasure, talking out loud, groaning, or sighing.

God knew the power and value of spoken contemplative worship when He commanded Joshua:

> "This Book of the Law *shall not depart from your mouth*, but you shall meditate in it day and night, that you may observe to do according to all that is written in it. For then you will make your way prosperous, and then you will have good success" (Joshua 1: 8, NKJV, emphasis added).

The word *hagah* in Psalm 1 describes the blessed man who delights in the law of the LORD:

> "But his delight is in the law of the LORD, and in His law he meditates day and night" (Psalm 1: 2 NKJV).

Receiving Truth in the Inner Man

Siyach and *Hagah* also mean "to ruminate". Our English words "muse, ponder, and meditate" also convey this meaning. When you ruminate, you think about something very deeply. You are "chewing the cud", which means turning something over and over to extract all the nutrients. Cows and sheep fill their stomachs with grass and then settle down quietly. The food is first softened and ingested and then they bring it up to chew it again. This process is repeated until all the nutrition has been extracted and absorbed into their system. The end result is creamy milk! What a helpful picture of Biblical meditation; it is the digestive system of the soul. Jeremiah wrote:

> "Your words were found and I ate them. And Your word was to me the joy and rejoicing of my heart: For I am called by Your name, O Lord of hosts" (Jeremiah 15: 16 NKJV).

It is not enough to hear and read the Word of God, we need to receive and *ruminate on* the Word until it is digested and becomes part of our being (1 Thessalonians 2: 13). The inner man must receive the truth.

Meditation is the process of taking in essential spiritual food. What the digestion of natural food is to the body, Biblical meditation is to the body, soul and spirit. The Word passes backwards and forwards from the spirit to the soul (mind, will and emotions), releasing its nutrients that provide counsel and understanding about God and His ways. Even our physical body benefits (Proverbs 3: 8). In this ever deepening cycle of meditation, God's Word is imparted, implanted, digested and engrafted—two different elements becoming one (Hebrews 8: 10; James 1: 21). The inner man—our spirit man— grows in stature, strength and ability. Our spiritual capacity is significantly increased.

In other words, the Holy Spirit takes the written Word and applies it, giving life to our inner being. Our minds are renewed to think God's way and we are transformed!

> "It is the Spirit who gives life, the flesh profits nothing. The words that I speak to you are spirit and they are life" (John 6: 63 NKJV).

Practicing the Presence of God

Biblical meditation transports us (body, soul and spirit) into His presence where He is the sole object of our adoration and worship. This is our true vocation in life. Of course, in His presence we discover irrepressible joy, unconditional love, ready and practical help, warm comfort, easy-to-understand wisdom, steadfast peace, renewed strength, available healing, abundant grace, strong protection, and every other provision for life we could ever wish for. There can be no greater blessing than to enter the presence of Almighty God!

During this discipleship season, we expect to grow in our love and desire for God and His Word. This is what Jesus refers to as hungering and thirsting for righteousness. Biblical meditation also develops in us a good attitude towards the Bible. The Word will become precious and our awareness of God's presence will increase. God loves our friendship and desires that we grow in our love for Him.

Paul Wilbur wrote the beautiful song, "In Your presence".

Chorus:
> In Your presence that's where I am strong. In Your presence, O Lord my God. In Your presence that's where I belong, seeking Your face touching Your grace, in the cleft of the Rock—in Your presence, O God.

1. I want to go where the rivers cannot overflow me, where my feet are on the Rock. I want to hide where the blazing fire cannot burn me, in Your presence, O God.
2. I want to hide where the flood of Evil cannot reach me, where I'm covered by the blood. I want to be where the schemes of darkness cannot touch me, in Your presence, O God.
3. You are my firm foundation I trust in You all day long. I am Your child and Your servant and You are my Strength and my song. You're my song.

© 1995 Integrity's Hosanna! Music

Prayer

Lord, thank You for creating me with the ability to meditate on You. O that I might draw near as I ponder Your works, divine Word, character and nature. I long for a deeper relationship with You. I need Your insight, wisdom, strength and direction. Amen.

Questions to Consider and Answer

- When your mind is relaxed, what do you enjoy thinking about? Where do your thoughts go? About what or of whom do think most of the time?
- Which subject is least enjoyable to think about? What do you avoid thinking about?
- God thinks. But what does God think about? Use a concordance to search the Scriptures and find out.

Life Group

1. Review the above questions and your answers. Allow a time of sharing.

2. Meditate on this Scripture together.

   "O, how I love your law! I meditate on it all day long. Your commands are always with me and make me wiser than my enemies. I have more insight than all my teachers, for I meditate on Your statutes. I have more understanding than the elders, for I obey Your precepts" (Psalm 119: 97-100 NKJV).

   As a group, observe *the process* of meditation (Appendix 2), taking into account what you have learned about the two Hebrew words, *siyach* and *hagah*.

- Read the Scripture at least five times. Let different people in the group read it out loud.

- Read it again, this time placing the emphasis on "I" and "Your".

- What are the benefits of God's Word according to these verses?

- Ask the Holy Spirit to lead and teach as you spend 10 minutes quietly meditating *(siyach)* on these verses.

   Remember, you are engaging in contemplation and reflection, focusing your thoughts on God. You are reflecting and pondering, chewing the verses over and over. You are exercising yourself in Biblical meditation.

- Having spent 10 minutes of quiet meditation, now spend another 10 minutes meditating, this time adding the other dimension of meditation (*hagah*):

  a. Muse (it implies spoken worship), murmur with pleasure; talk out loud to the Lord and each other about what you are gleaning. You may groan as God awakens feeling, sigh with satisfaction, or speak out praise or revelation.
  b. Turn the verse into a song or a poem using your own words; sing it or read it back to the Lord and/or each other.

3. Describe to the group what the Scripture now means to you.

4. Let each turn the Scripture, thoughts, impressions and new understanding into a prayer of thanksgiving and praise.

5. Before you leave, make sure you know the date and time of your next life group meeting and which chapter you are to prepare.

CHAPTER THREE

Understanding our Make-up

"When you were born-again, you received the mind of Christ."
— Andrew Wommack

It is a special day when someone turns his/her life over to Jesus, repenting and believing His blood atoned for his/her sins. Nevertheless, what happens next? In the spiritually hostile arena of life, that precious decision made in a moment of sincere surrender, is severely tested. Unsure of what this new life in Jesus means, a battle unfolds as the patterns and ways of the old life seek to regain ground. It is a fierce battle against the temptations of the old familiar sinful ways. Too many who started well fall away from faith in God. So:

- How do we maintain an intimate relationship with the Lord?
- How do we find direction for our new life?
- How do we strengthen ourselves in the faith?
- How do we stand in righteousness when faced with crookedness and deceit?
- How do we keep our mind pure when bombarded daily with lurid images, coarse language and filthy humour?
- How do we become confident in knowing right from wrong?

God uses the powerful combination of His Spirit and His

Word to develop in us inner strength and victory over temptation. Biblical meditation is the means by which the Holy Spirit integrates the Word into our hearts with encouraging and fruitful results. It is a process of spiritual growth. The Psalmist says:

> "Your word I have hidden in my heart that I might not sin against You. Blessed are You, O LORD!" (Ps 119: 11-12 NKJV)

From the Beginning

Why is Biblical meditation so powerful? Why is it a healing medicine to our body, soul and spirit? How does it create the life of God in us? As we look at how God has made us, what went wrong in disobedience and how God sorted out our mess, we will appreciate the vital part that meditation upon God and His Word plays.

God created man to be His family (Ephesians 3: 15). Adam and Eve enjoyed a close-knit relationship with Him, and with each other. They were one—complete. God lovingly cared for man, offering provision, protection, partnership and opportunity. In return, man loved and enjoyed God with all his heart and strength; he willingly depended on Him for all things. From the beginning of time, man fed on the words and ways of His Creator, eating and drinking from his only source of true life. As he set his thoughts and heart on God, he experienced open and edifying communication, close fellowship and friendship. Man delighted in God and would live, move and have his being in his Creator (Acts 17: 28). God was everything and His majesty filled man's heart and mind. He was the all-consuming focus of man's meditation.

> "Everyone who is called by My name, whom I have created for My glory; I have formed him, yes, I have made him" (Isaiah 43: 7 NKJV).

35

Made in the Image of God

God made man in a particular way. God, Himself a three-person being, made man in His image in three dimensions with body, soul, and spirit. These three form the human being. We are fearfully and wonderfully made (Psalm 139: 14).

> "Now may the God of peace sanctify you completely; and may your whole spirit, soul and body be preserved blameless, at the coming of our Lord Jesus Christ" (1 Thessalonians 5: 23 NKJV).

Most of us know that we have a body, soul and spirit. The **body** is our physical body. The **soul** has three dimensions—mind, will and emotions. However, what is our **spirit** up to?

- The **mind** formulates beliefs and values, suggesting possible courses of action.
- Our **will** determines whether we do, behave or act in certain ways.
- Our **emotions** reveal what is happening on the inside, whether it is positive or negative, happy or sad, depressed or encouraged.
- Our **body** communicates physical health (or otherwise) and provides practical function in response to the decision of the will.
- Our **spirit**, like the soul, cannot be seen or felt. Yet, it is also a real part of us and shows itself as an aspect of our unique being. It is the part which God created with the ability to connect with God (1 Corinthians 2: 10-14). It is what has been deposited in our spirit that defines who we are and gives us identity (1 Peter 3: 4).

God Formed Man

Our body was formed from the dust of the earth, clay moulded by Father's hands, like clay on a potter's wheel. God placed within our body a **soul**, (mind, will and emotions) enabling us to freely think, choose and feel. In the beginning, before sin entered the world, God breathed His life into man's **spirit** and he became a living soul.

> "And the Lord God formed man from the dust of the ground, and breathed into his nostrils the breath of life and man became a living being (Genesis 2: 7 NKJV).

> Then God said: "Let us make man in Our image, according to Our likeness". So God created man in His own image; male and female He created them" (Genesis 1: 26-27 NKJV).

When God breathed the breath of life into man, amazingly, God connected His Spirit with man. A life-supporting "umbilical cord" was created, connecting God's Spirit to man's spirit, and thus man had open access to God. Therefore, in the beginning man's entire being was spiritually alive, because the breath of God was in him. However, we know that this changed when Adam sinned. His sinful action severed the spirit-connection with God; he instantaneously became spiritually dead.

Three Diagrams to Consider

The following diagrams illustrate what happened:

In the Beginning before Sin - Diagram 1

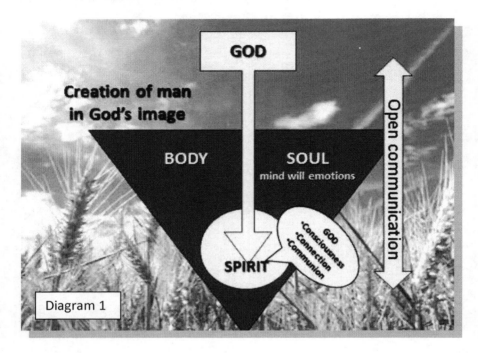

Before sin entered the world through disobedience, man enjoyed an open channel of love, communication and fellowship with Almighty God—spirit to Spirit. God is Spirit (John 4: 24) and man's relationship with God was in the Spirit. It was the most intimate of all relationships. Later, God described such a union of spirits in the context of marriage—the intimate joining of two into one. Man's spirit was God-conscious; he knew God by his spirit. He also knew God's voice and God spoke freely with him. Fellowship with God was rich communion. Man was healthy, body, soul and spirit.

Sin Entered the World - Diagram 2:

We do not know how long such bliss continued, but we do know there came a day of mayhem and devastation. God entrusted the Garden of Eden to Adam and Eve with the command that from one tree—the tree of knowledge of good and evil—they were not allowed to eat. God said that if they ate from the forbidden tree, they would "surely die". God did not say, "You *might* die"; He said they *would surely die* and it would be *in that day*. Eve gave in to the temptation to "be like God", and ate the fruit of the forbidden tree. Adam followed suit.

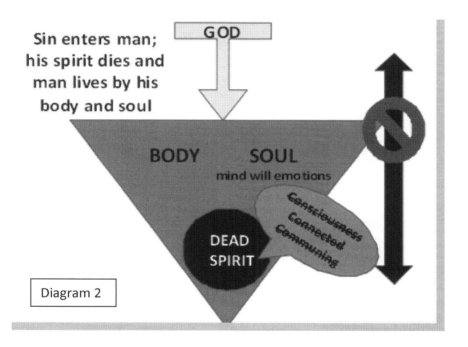

Sin enters man; his spirit dies and man lives by his body and soul

GOD

BODY   SOUL
mind will emotions

DEAD SPIRIT

Consciousness
Connected
Communing

Diagram 2

> "Then the LORD God took the man and put him in the Garden of Eden to tend and keep it. And the LORD God commanded the man, saying, "Of every tree of the garden you may freely eat; but of the tree of the knowledge of good and evil you shall not eat, for in the day that you eat of it you shall surely die""" (Genesis 2: 15-17 NKJV).

Adam and Eve certainly did not die physically "in that day". Adam lived for eight hundred years (Genesis 5: 4). So, what did God mean by saying, "you shall surely die"? What died? The moment they disobeyed God their **spirits** died—the part that connected them to God—their life-support channel. Instead of experiencing open and free God-consciousness, they were left only with *self*-consciousness (Genesis 3: 8). The absence of Spirit-life brought spiritual death. God's Spirit was no longer *within* them; they were devoid of the breath of God. From that time forward their offspring would be born in their likeness—spiritually dead (without the life of God), self-centred and self-motivated in body, soul and spirit. Due to the absence of the inner presence of God in man, the evil deeds of men increased. Wickedness of every description increased to the point that God wished He had never created man! Look at what God said:

> "Then the LORD saw that the wickedness of man was great in the earth, and that every intent of the thoughts of his heart was only evil continually. And the LORD was sorry that He had made man on the earth, and He was grieved in His heart. So the LORD said, "I will destroy man whom I have created from the face of the earth, both man and beast, creeping thing and birds of the air, for I am sorry that I have made them"" (Genesis 6: 5-7 NKJV).

There was no holding back evil—God's righteous breath was absent—there was no divine restraint in man. The Light inside had gone out. What a tragedy and what devastating consequences for humankind. A holy God could not dwell where sin prevailed. Of course, they had natural breath to live physically, but the Spirit-breath of God no longer was present. Inner contentment that accompanied belonging to God was lost. With intimacy sacrificed, the absence of Life brought immediate death. It was over.

Disobedience to the command of God had severed man's spirit from God's, and sin was born in the world for the first time. All men would be born in sin and die in sin, separate from God. Every child born would be spiritually dead—devoid of the life of God.

The Redeemer Comes - Diagram 3

"Who were born, not of blood nor of the will of the flesh, nor of the will of man, but of God" (John 1: 13 NKJV).

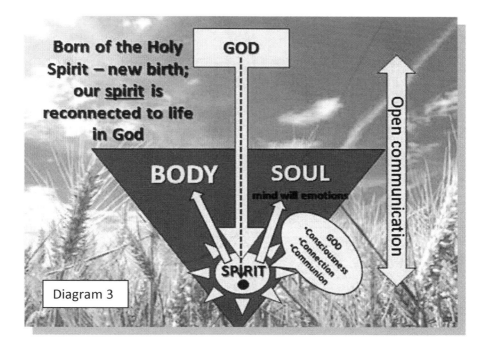

Thankfully, the story does not end in such hopelessness because the promised Redeemer is coming! God told Satan, the accuser, that He would send someone to defeat him. One day, the Seed of a woman would redeem the sin of all humankind, restoring God-consciousness, connection to God and communion with God.

The following verse is a most remarkable prophecy. It looked down the centuries to the day when Jesus would be born of the Holy Spirit in Mary's womb—the womb of a virgin. The masculine pronoun indicates that the fulfilment of this promise would be a man, born of the seed of a woman. God faithfully sent the Redeemer, His only Son Jesus, into the world to bring eternal redemption.

> "And I will put enmity between you and the woman, and between your seed and her seed: He shall bruise you on the head, and you shall bruise him on the heel" (Genesis 3: 15 NKJV).

Jesus Lays Down His Life

> "The next day John saw Jesus coming toward him, and said, "Behold! *The Lamb of God* who takes away the sin of the world" (John 1: 29 NKJV, emphasis added).

> "I am the good shepherd; and I know My sheep, and am known by My own. As the Father knows Me, even so I know the Father; and I lay down My life for the sheep. And other sheep I have which are not of this fold; them also I must bring, and they will hear My voice; and there will be one flock and one shepherd. Therefore, My Father loves Me, because I lay down My life that I may take it again. No one takes it from Me, but I lay it down of Myself. I have power to lay it down, and I have power to take it again. This command I have received from My Father" (John 10: 14-18 NKJV).

Every year, at the Feast of Passover, Israel celebrated God's redemption from the slavery and bondage of Egypt. The Israelites brought lambs, without blemish, to the temple in Jerusalem to be sacrificed. It was commanded by God—blood must be shed for the remission of sins (Hebrews 9: 22). However, there came a very significant Passover, a world-shaking moment when God provided a perfect sin-offering in His Son Jesus—the Lamb of God; His blood would be shed to redeem the world (Genesis 22: 8; Romans 6: 10).

As Passover lambs were slain in the temple, outside of the walls of Jerusalem, on a Roman cross, God's Lamb was being slain, redeeming the world from the slavery and bondage of sin. Jesus, Redeemer of humankind, voluntarily laid down His life, taking the punishment of death we justly deserved for our sins.

Since the shed blood of Jesus on the cross, it became possible through repentance for man to be reconciled to God, reconnecting man's spirit to God's Spirit (Colossians 1: 20; Romans 5: 10; 2 Corinthians 5: 18; Hebrews 9: 11-14). However, man must be born-again to be reconciled.

Nicodemus—Born Again by the Spirit

Nicodemus, a Pharisee, was a religious man well-versed in the Scriptures. However, his knowledge did not produce life; his spirit was dead. He knew a lot about God and performed service and works for God, but had no living relationship with God.

> "Nicodemus asked Jesus: "How can a man be born when he is old? He cannot enter a second time into his mother's womb and be born, can he?" Jesus answered him: "Truly, truly I say to you, unless one is born of water and the spirit, he cannot enter the Kingdom of God"" (John 3: 4 NKJV).

We are born naturally of water, but we must also be born supernaturally of the Spirit of God to be born-again. Many new believers say, "When I received Jesus into my heart it was as if I made a brand new start". They did, they were born anew as spiritual babes; spiritual life had just begun. Just as with Mary, the mother of Jesus, in conception, the Holy Spirit overshadows our dead spirit and gives us new birth. Our dead spirit comes to life!

Connection and Communion Restored

At Passover, Jesus made atonement for sin. Fifty days later, on the Day of Pentecost (Acts 2: 1), God poured out His Spirit. "Pentecost" simply means "fifty". During this 50-day harvest period, the Jews not only celebrated the ingathering of the harvest, but also, significantly, celebrated the giving of the Law to Moses on Mount Sinai—God's divine instruction and teaching.

With intention and perfect timing, God laid His Lamb on the cross at Passover and poured out the promised Holy Spirit at Pentecost (Acts 2: 21), fulfilling the prophecies of Joel 2: 32 and Jeremiah 31: 31-34. The outpouring of the Holy Spirit sealed the New Covenant cut with the blood of Jesus (2 Corinthians 1: 22; Ephesians 1: 13; Ephesians 4: 30). Now, instead of having the Law of God written on tablets of stone, the Holy Spirit would put God's Law in minds and write it on hearts. Paul describes it as transformation by the renewing of your mind (Romans 12: 1-2).

The New Covenant gloriously fulfils the feasts of Passover and Pentecost. We are born-again of the Spirit and reconciled to God—represented in the Feast of Passover, and filled with His life-giving Spirit—represented in the Feast of Pentecost.

Look again at diagram 3. In the New Covenant God restored _inner_ God-consciousness and intimate communion with Him, and gave dynamic power to reign in life, overcoming sin. We are once again connected to God, spirit to Spirit, and are wholly dependent on the breath of God—the Holy Spirit—to live and walk in a manner pleasing to our Father.

Tragically, many believers who are suspicious, afraid or

ignorant of the fullness of the Spirit experience forgiveness of sins but live trying to please God through self-effort—in their own strength. What started well in the Spirit (new birth) continued in the flesh (Galatians 3: 3). Therefore, we exhort you to ask God, our heavenly Father, to fill you with His precious Spirit. We are commanded, "Be filled with the Holy Spirit" (Ephesians 5: 18).

Spirit-filled and Spirit-led

God has appointed the Holy Spirit to team up with His living Word to deliver life to our body, soul and spirit, and lead them into truth, healing and freedom! Biblical meditation is the conduit. However, what happens in those for whom this is not the reality? Instead of being led by the Holy Spirit and God's Word they are led, counselled and guided by their body, soul and spirit with tragic spiritual consequences. Depending on which aspect dominates—body, soul (mind, will, emotions) or spirit, they are misled and deceived in life.

Led by our Body

When we allow the **body** to lead and not the Holy Spirit, the choice of what we do, or not do is primarily dictated by physical needs—comfort, cravings, desires, disability. Led by the Holy Spirit we will accomplish many things despite weakness.

Led by our Mind

Led by our **mind** and not by the Holy Spirit we detour into rationalism and error. The **mind** will always put up "reasoned" resistance to repentance and the cross. The person controlled by his/her mind resists repentance and change because he/she rationalises sin. The mind dictates that free choice permits any sort of behaviour, change is not necessary, and argues that science contradicts Scripture. If we are headstrong in belief and decision-making, we are misled.

Led by our Will

The **will** executes what the mind, emotion, human spirit or Holy Spirit dictates; it can lead us into, or away from, the will of God. It is a strong leader and causes man to be stubborn. Therefore, on a daily basis, it is very important to submit our **will** to the will of God. With the permission of our **will** (in our soul), the Holy Spirit can harness our spirit to God's Word as truth and lead us on into abundant spiritual life.

Led by Emotion

Led by **emotion** and not by the Holy Spirit we are steered by our feelings, inevitably in the wrong direction. Instead of guidance by the principles and truth of God's Word, Satan masterfully manipulates strong or weak feelings to direct and even control us. Satan exploits our tendency to live by the "feel good" standard of the contemporary world or what we "feel to be right" according to our mood.

The evidence of this is in the changes in national laws with regard to marriage and euthanasia. Feelings may run high and a powerful case presented, but emotions are not necessarily in line with God's Word! Emotions are important and helpful communicators, but they are an extremely dangerous prophet or dictator, especially when they are contrary to the Word of God. We are to control our emotions, not allowing them to become our taskmasters.

Led by our Human Spirit

Led by our **human spirit** (without the Holy Spirit and spiritually dead) we are open to all sorts of other deceptive spirits—evil spirits contrary to the Spirit of God. Rather than choosing to resist temptation and walk in victory by the power of the Holy Spirit, we choose sin, darkness and death.

When our **human spirit** is devoid of the light and life of the

Holy Spirit and God's Word, we leave ourselves open to spiritualist and occult influences. We may feel disturbed, angry, confused, panic-stricken and anxious. Therefore, repentance may also necessitate prayer for deliverance from evil spirits. However, be warned, the enemy may put up a strong and loud resistance; he does not want to give up territory or control.

Led by the Holy Spirit

In life we are to be led by the **Holy Spirit** and He always leads according to God's Word (Ephesians 6: 17). Fully connected and alive to God, our spirit is now one with the Holy Spirit. We are both enabled and instructed how to "walk in the Spirit" (Galatians 5: 16), "live in the Spirit" (Galatians 5: 25), "purpose in the Spirit" (Acts 19: 21), "pray in the Spirit" (Ephesians 6: 18), "worship God in the Spirit" (Philippians 3: 3), "love in the Spirit" (Colossians 1: 8). We are without excuse.

This is a 180-degree turn, because when God's Spirit was absent, our soul and body led us into danger. Formerly a selfish mind, emotions with no anchor, a proud will and a complaining body influenced the choices we made. These three, without the renewing or the restraint of the Spirit of God, led us into fleshly attitudes and behaviour. Paul put it this way:

> "But you are not in the flesh but in the Spirit, if indeed the Spirit of God dwells in you. Now if anyone does not have the Spirit of Christ, he is not His. And if Christ is in you, the body is dead because of sin, but the Spirit is life because of righteousness. But if the Spirit of Him who raised Jesus from the dead dwells in you, He who raised Christ from the dead will also give life to your mortal bodies through His Spirit who dwells in you" (Romans 8: 9-11 NKJV).

The deposit of God's Word through Biblical meditation keeps our body, soul and spirit healthy and purposeful. Regular Word-exercise ensures that we maintain clean and open channels of communication with God.

> "On the last day, that great day of the feast, Jesus stood and cried out, saying, "If anyone thirsts, let him come to Me and drink. He who believes in Me, as the Scripture has said, out of his heart will flow rivers of living water"" (John 7: 37-38 NKJV).

Prayer

Loving Father, You have turned my life around and made me spiritually alive. Thank you for putting Your Word in my mind and on my heart by the Holy Spirit. Your Presence is with and in me. Teach and train me to walk, live, pray and worship in the Spirit. Help me to grasp what it is to be led by the Holy Spirit. Help me to recognise when I am being misled by my human spirit, emotions or mind. Amen.

Questions to Consider and Answer

- What or who guides your life—your human spirit, emotions, mind or Holy Spirit? Try to think about events and experiences of the last month. What or who influenced the decisions you made, and with what result?
- Which Bible stories or personal examples illustrate the lessons of this chapter? For example, think about the life of King David and identify what or who guided him at different times. What about Jonah? You may like to choose another Bible character like Abraham, Jacob, Moses, Paul or Peter.

Write your answers in your journal and explain how you came to those conclusions.

Life Group

1. How did you answer the question, "what or who guides your life—your human spirit, emotions, mind or Holy Spirit?

   a. Share examples or stories.

2. Discuss what it means to be led by the Spirit.

   a. What does it involve? How would you explain "walking in the Spirit" to a new believer?
   b. How have you been led by the Spirit?

3. Close in prayer. Take time to repent of any areas where you have denied God His rightful place in your lives. Consciously lay your lives down (body, soul and spirit) before Him. Make it an act of sincere dedication. Pray particularly that God would fill each one with His Spirit.

Scripture for Meditation

"It is the Spirit who gives life; the flesh profits nothing. The words that I speak to you are spirit, and they are life" (John 6: 63 NKJV).

CHAPTER FOUR

Renewal of the Mind

"When a Christian walks like an unbeliever, they get
the same results—death. Believers who don't
understand and apply the knowledge of God in their
lives gravitate toward carnal mindedness."
    —Andrew Wommack

"I beseech you therefore, brethren, by the mercies of
God, that you present your bodies a living sacrifice,
holy, acceptable to God, which is your reasonable
service. And do not be conformed to this world, but
be transformed by the renewing of your mind, that you may
prove what is that good and acceptable and perfect
will of God" (Romans 12: 1-2 NKJV, emphasis
added).

Each chapter of this study builds on the foundation laid in previous
chapters. We have considered the devastating effects of sin on our
body, soul and spirit. We have also considered God's redemptive
plan for our body, soul and spirit in the New Covenant, cut with the
blood of Jesus. Now, in the next three chapters we consider the role

of Biblical meditation in the transformation of our lives. Transformation of body, soul and spirit happen when we:

1.   Lay down our lives.
Paul says that the right response to the "mercies of God" (Romans 12: 1) revealed in His plan of salvation (Romans 1-11), is that we too, willingly sacrifice our lives as a praise offering to God. We give all to Him.

2.   Put off the old life and put on the new life.
This is a decision we make as we fully embrace the new life offered in Christ Jesus, closing the door on the "old life"—old patterns of thinking and behaviour. We leave the kingdom of darkness and enter the kingdom of light.

3.   Take responsibility to renew our minds in God's Word.
We are to apply ourselves in putting off our negative and corrupt thinking and putting on God's thoughts. This means that we repent of sinful and self-centred patterns of thought, and consciously "put on" the mind of Christ (2 Corinthians 10: 5).

God's Thoughts are Higher

We have taken up our new position in Christ Jesus. With Him, we are

raised up and are seated in heavenly places (Ephesians 2: 6). From this highest seat of glory and power our view of life and the position from which we live, utterly changes. We now see and live from God's high and holy perspective. We were earthly-minded, but now we are heavenly-minded, God-minded and Kingdom-minded. Our mind is "set on things above, not on things on the earth" (Colossians 3: 2). Accepting that change of position enables us to choose what delights God over what pleases our flesh. Renewal of the mind requires a conscious mind-shift from earth to heaven. Believers must accept that their lives run contraflow to the trends of life and the life-style of many of their friends.

Wrong Thinking and Attitudes

In Romans 12 and 13 the Apostle Paul elaborates on the type of thoughts and attitudes which need to be renewed.

1. Thinking of ourselves more highly than we ought
2. Having an exaggerated opinion of our own importance
3. Independent thinking
4. Superficial and insincere love
5. Loving what God defines as evil
6. Lethargy in spiritual matters
7. Impatience in suffering and tribulation
8. Prayerlessness
9. Stinginess and selfishness
10. Disparaging others
11. Snobbishness and exclusive attitudes
12. Proud attitude
13. Vengeful attitude
14. Attitude of superiority, lording it over others
15. Rebellious attitude towards authority
16. Unfriendly attitude

The Mind of Christ

What is the mind of Christ?

- The mind of Christ is love, joy (gladness), peace, patience (an even temper, forbearance), kindness, goodness (benevolence), faithfulness, gentleness (meekness, humility), self-control (self-restraint) (Galatians 5: 22-23). These are the *"fruit of the Spirit"*.
- The mind of Christ is love: love is patient and kind; love does not envy or boast; it is not arrogant or rude; does not insist on its own way; is not irritable or resentful; does not rejoice in wrongdoing, but rejoices with the truth. Love bears all things, believes all things, hopes all things, endures all things (1 Corinthians 13: 4-7).
- The mind of Christ is godly and content (1 Timothy 6: 6-10).
- The mind of Christ is stable and peaceful (Philippians 4: 6-7).
- The mind of Christ is true, honourable, just, pure, lovely, commendable, excellent, and praiseworthy (Philippians 4: 8).
- The mind of Christ is humble, meek, righteous, pure, and makes peace—it reconciles (Matthew 5: 3-10).

Be assured, we have the mind of Christ. It is ours through faith in Christ Jesus. However, we must lay hold of it by resolutely turning away from patterns of sinful thought and allowing the Holy Spirit to nurture the engrafted thought patterns and attitudes of Christ Jesus. This takes time, effort and discipline, but the rewards are wonderful. Spend some moments meditating on the following Scriptures and note what strikes you.

- Have this mind among yourselves, which is yours in Christ Jesus (Philippians 2: 5).
- Be renewed in the spirit of your minds … (Ephesians 4: 23).
- Put on the new self, which is being renewed in knowledge after the image of its creator (Colossians 3: 10).
- Do not lose heart. Though our outer self is wasting away, our inner self is being renewed day by day (2 Corinthians 4: 16).

- Sanctify them in the truth; your word is truth (John 17: 17).
- And you will know the truth, and the truth will set you free (John 8: 31-32).

False Beliefs

Our mind formulates our beliefs and values (whether faulty or otherwise), based on the instruction and influence of authority figures (whether false or true "prophets") and on our life experiences. Consequently, our beliefs and values determine our attitudes and behaviour. If our beliefs and values are flawed, our thinking and decision-making will be unsound too. The mind does not act in isolation: what we think affects how we feel (emotions), and in turn directs, for good or ill, the choices we make (will). In the past, our thought patterns misdirected both our feelings and actions.

> "To the pure, all things are pure, but to the defiled
> and unbelieving, nothing is pure; but both their minds
> and their consciences are defiled" (Titus 1: 15 NKJV).

Here are some examples of experiences, which form deceptive beliefs and values:

1. Perhaps, as a child we lost contact with our mother in a shopping centre for an hour or so. This traumatic experience of abandonment could have been stored as a memory that says, "I am abandoned. There is no one to take care of me and I have to take care of myself". Later on, should we experience a similar situation, this stored belief of the lie of being abandoned, surfaces as a "voice" telling us that there is no one looking out for us, not even God. Satan has managed to lodge this lie in our heart. Consequently, we believe God has also abandoned us and feel cut off from His help/presence.

The Word of God says, *"I will never leave you nor forsake you"* (Hebrews 13: 5).

2. Intimidation is a spirit that attaches itself to past wounds and pain. How many of us are subject to intimidation, living like a puppet on someone's string? We cower, avoid and hide away in fear, adapting to its menacing control. Rather than being led by the Holy Spirit, intimidation and fear dictate what, when and how we do things. How many times has this thwarted God's plans for our lives?

   The Word of God says, *"I have not given you a spirit of fear, but of power and of love and of a sound mind"* (2 Timothy 1: 7).

3. Parents, who often criticise and seldom praise their children, instil in them a sense of inferiority and rejection. This establishes the lie that performance determines value/worth. This results in a mind-set that says, "I'll never be good enough; I'm not worth anything".

   The Word of God says, *"I am fearfully and wonderfully made; marvellous are Your works"* (Psalm 139: 14; Ephesians 1: 6).

4. At the other end of the scale, when children are reared to believe that they are superior to others, they develop an inflated ego. They come to believe that they are God's gift to the church/world etc., that without them nothing would happen.

   The Word of God says, *"For I say, through the grace given to me, to everyone who is among you, not to think of himself more highly than he ought to think, but to think soberly , as God has dealt to each one a measure of faith"* (Romans 12: 3).

5. Growing up in an environment of material lack may cause a child to believe that there is never enough to take care of his/her needs, and that God does not care or provide. This may result in a stingy mind-set that says, "I have to hold onto what I have". Of course, this will be reflected in our giving to others.

    The Word of God says, *"But this I say: He who sows sparingly will also reap sparingly, and he who sows bountifully will also reap bountifully. So let each one give as he purposes in his heart, not grudgingly or of necessity; for God loves a cheerful giver. And God is able to make all grace abound toward you, that you, always having all sufficiency in all things, may have an abundance for every good work"* (2 Corinthians 9: 6-9).

6. A child, who wasn't taught to face and tackle difficulties and challenges, grows up to believe that he is a helpless victim of his circumstances.

    The Word of God says, *"I can do all things through Christ who strengthens me* (Philippians 4: 13 NKJV).

Recognising Deceptive Beliefs and Values

From time to time, we all still suffer the defeat of recurring old thought patterns and behaviour. We seem to be dragged back into patterns from which we have been freed. We should recognise that these patterns are spiritual in nature and that they form well-established arguments, which set themselves up against the true knowledge of God. Satan wants to keep our minds locked into sinful thought patterns. However, if we take every thought captive to the obedience of Christ Jesus, our minds and our lives will continue to be changed. Paul describes it clearly.

> "For the weapons of our warfare are not carnal but mighty in God for pulling down strongholds, casting down arguments

and every high thing that exalts itself against the knowledge of God, bringing every thought into captivity to the obedience of Christ, and being ready to punish all disobedience when your obedience is fulfilled" (2 Corinthians 10: 3-6 NKJV).

Paul realised that the renewal of the mind has to be intentional:

"We *take captive every thought* to make it obedient to Christ" (2 Corinthians 10: 5 NKJV, emphasis added).

In the Message this passage is paraphrased as:

"Tearing down barriers erected against the truth of God, fitting every loose thought and emotion and impulse into the structure of life shaped by Christ."

King David understood God's way of renewal—truth must penetrate the heart, not simply rest in the mind as knowledge. He cried out for change:

"Behold, You desire truth *in the inward parts*, and in the hidden part *You will make me to know* wisdom" (Psalm 51: 6, NKJV, emphasis added)

He realised that self-help, and positive thinking would not answer the cry of a sinful heart; the planting of truth is required in our inmost parts to bring about change.

God Joins Himself to Us

In the New Covenant, a blood covenant, God promises to put His Law (His principles, precepts, statutes, instructions, and commandments) in our minds and write it on our hearts (Jeremiah 31: 31-34). Why is that so important? It is a covenant transaction.

The Word is God, so by putting the Word of God in our

minds and on our hearts, God is literally promising commitment in marriage terms: "I am joining Myself to you. All that I am and have is yours. You are Mine". When truth about God—His character, nature and His loving ways—is so embedded, we come to think and act just like He does! How is this possible? It is a supernatural work of love and grace, performed by the Holy Spirit.

We are the temple of the Holy Spirit (1 Corinthians 6: 19); we house Him. Consequently, God is no longer distant, He is within and we intimately know Him (John 17: 3). In a most wonderful way, Biblical meditation awakens our body, soul and spirit to the presence of God.

Prerequisites for Renewing the Mind

1. **Humility**. Renewing of the mind requires that we be humble and teachable. God resists the proud.

2. **Revering the Word of God.** We must revere the Bible as the unchanging Word of God—the final authority on all matters. In 2 Timothy 3: 16 we are reminded that *all* Scripture (even the passages we have chosen not to believe) is given by inspiration of God, and is profitable for doctrine, for reproof, for correction, for instruction in righteousness, that the man of God may be complete, thoroughly equipped for every good work. We must position ourselves as a diligent student of the Word (2 Timothy 2: 15).

3. **The presence of the Holy Spirit**. The Holy Spirit guides us in all truth (John 16: 13). He takes up His sword, "the sword of the Spirit"—God's Word—cuts to the quick and lays bare what hinders us from receiving new life (Ephesians 6: 17). Once these hindrances are exposed, He leads us to repentance and wholeness. In Hebrews 4: 12 it says that the Word of God is so

precise that it can divide between soul and spirit, bone and marrow. It is also a discerner of the thoughts and intentions of the heart (Hebrews 4: 13). This is exactly what we need, because we cannot see or discern heart matters for ourselves (Jeremiah 17: 9-10). In His light we see light (Psalm 36: 9).

4. **Obedience**. We are to be absolutely obedient to God's Word. When God says, "put off the old man and put on the new", we do it. When God says, "be filled with the Spirit", we earnestly seek to be filled. When Jesus says, "Forsake the world, take up your cross and follow me", we do just that. This even means obedience to parts of the Word that our church traditions have chosen to lay aside.

5. **Worship in Spirit and in truth (John 4: 23-24).** Worship in Spirit and truth achieves three things: a) It focuses our mind on God, away from ourselves, b) it causes Satan to flee and c) it opens our mind and heart to receive the mind and heart of God.

Something very beautiful happens when our body, soul and spirit connect and commune with Him. It is as if we have access to an open heaven where we meet Him face to face.

A True Story: The Road Home

Jasmine was in a trance as she drove home. Oblivious to the heavy traffic, a million thoughts raced relentlessly through her tense and shocked mind. Her doctor had just diagnosed her with liver cancer. It was the worst news, her life was being cut short. She registered no junctions or lights as thoughts flooded her mind: "What about Clint, what about my girls, what about my beautiful grandchildren? How will I cope? Who will help me? Should I ask God to heal me? What if He says no?" There were far more questions than answers. It wasn't fair; there was still so much to live for.

For several months since she received the news, dark thoughts of impending death ambushed her mind. A deep depression had descended like a fog. Surely, her faith would hold her steady. Shouldn't there be a sense of joy as she anticipated heaven? No joy, no stability; her mind was plagued with incessant doubts about life and death. Her heart was devoid of strength and courage; she had entered the darkest tunnel of her life.

Desperately, she paged through her address book. Whom could she trust with her pain? Finally, her mind turned to Mintie Nel. Perhaps it was a natural choice because Mintie, who suffers from a chronic illness, knows what it takes to overcome and endure. There is not a day in her life without swollen joints, acute pain and stiffness; just getting out of bed is a daily challenge. One suspects, that it was also Mintie's spiritual verve, steadiness and peaceful disposition, which made her the chosen channel of hope. Jasmine telephoned with a long list of questions:

"How have you stayed so positive in the midst of pain?"

"What is your secret?"

"How can I have such assurance?"

"All I think about is what I am about to lose!"

"I don't know what to do, can you help me?"

"Mintie, why me?"

"Where does all this doubt and fear come from?"

She choked back the rising tide of emotion, which threatened to overwhelm her. Jasmine had entered the "valley of the shadow of death" (Psalm 23); suffering was to be her companion and friend on her road to heaven. This suffering was not the cross for which she had asked, but God had lovingly ordained it both for her good and for the good of those involved in her journey.

Listening intently to her caller, Mintie shared how the Lord strengthened and enabled her through Biblical meditation. "Jasmine, this is the key. It is the resurrection power of God through His Word which gives me what I need every day!" she said. "It is part of my daily routine to soak my mind in God's promises, allowing the Holy Spirit to deposit life-giving truth into my heart. That is how I get out of bed in the morning; God's Word transmits life to my body. The joy of Jesus is my strength."

It would have sounded trite from anyone other than Mintie. However, this was no theory; Biblical meditation provides her with the strength to overcome, it is her way of life. It is more than just a spiritual discipline; Mintie meets intimately with Jesus in His Word. Hungry and desperate, Jasmine soaked up every word of direction like a sponge.

Encouraged and inspired by what she had heard, Jasmine made Biblical meditation the priority of her day during the following months. As the Holy Spirit brought the promises in the Word to life in her heart, change began to happen. From the inside out, the Word and the Spirit supernaturally performed their transforming work. Heaviness and despair lifted and a new confidence and joy entered her heart. It sounds strange, but she began to thank the Lord for suffering, because the newfound intimacy with Jesus was so precious. She had fallen in love again with God and had found sterling courage and strength in His Word. Pessimistic and dark thoughts turned to optimism as the Word seeped into her spirit; she brimmed with a newfound hope. Death no longer filled her with fear, because rekindled love had replaced it.

Far from being quiet about the changes, Jasmine began to share her meditations with her family and friends. Naturally, they were vicariously suffering, but pretended they were not, wanting to be strong *for her*. The Word of God, through Jasmine, also revived them! This story does not end with a testimony of a miraculous healing. Jasmine still had liver cancer, but the liver cancer did not have her! She was no longer prisoner to the cancer; it no longer governed her life. Doubt and fear no longer ruled and dictated her thought patterns. She was being transformed.

Every day the practice of meditation brought her into the presence of Jesus and heaven filled her heart with joyful anticipation. Full of radiance, she passed away and entered the presence of the Lord. She had received the most complete and perfect healing. One day we will too!

Prayer

O Lord, I am in awe of You and Your ways. Help me to recognise each occasion when I entertain sinful thoughts and attitudes. Please renew my mind. I open my heart and mind to the Holy Spirit so that He may put truth in my mind and write it on my heart. I ask that truth will become a reality in me. Amen.

Scripture for Meditation

"But you have not so learned Christ, if indeed you have heard Him and have been taught by Him, as the truth is in Jesus: that you put off, concerning your former conduct, the old man which grows corrupt according to the deceitful lusts, and be renewed in the spirit of your mind, and that you put on the new man which was created according to God, in true righteousness and holiness" (Ephesians 4: 20-24 NKJV).

Questions to Consider

For many of us, spiritual growth slowed or stopped after we were born again, because we didn't understand that God wants to change the way we think. Old patterns of thought and unbelief act as barriers to knowing God. However, God desires that we be conformed to the image of his Son, Christ Jesus, by the renewal of our mind (Romans 8: 29).

- Luke 11: 13 says that our Father gives the Holy Spirit to those who ask.
- In the following Scripture what does God say He will give, and what does He say He will remove?

"Moreover, I will give you a new heart and put a new Spirit within you; and I will remove the heart of stone from your flesh and give you a heart of flesh. And I will put My Spirit within you" (Ezekiel 36: 26-27 NKJV)

- How has God fulfilled this promise in you?
- Rewrite this Scripture in your own words. Rephrase and personalise it, writing comments and notes in your journal.
- What changes have you seen in your thought patterns since you surrendered your life to Jesus? Summarise your spiritual progress.

Life Group Meditation Exercise

- Take time to review the impact of chapter 4 on your lives.
  - What key points affected you? What effect did they have?
  - Discuss any questions which arise.
- Take time to meditate on the following Scripture passage.

"He who dwells in the secret place of the Most High shall abide under the shadow of the Almighty. I will say of the LORD, "He is my refuge and my fortress; My God, in Him I will trust." Surely, He shall deliver you from the snare of the fowler and from the perilous pestilence. He shall cover you with His feathers, and under His wings you shall take refuge; His truth shall be your shield and buckler. You shall not be afraid of the terror by night, nor of the arrow that flies by day, nor of the pestilence that walks in darkness, nor of the destruction that lays waste at noonday. A thousand may fall at your side, and ten thousand at your right hand; but it shall not come near you. Only with your eyes shall you look, and see the reward of the wicked.

Because you have made the LORD, who is my refuge, even the Most High, your dwelling place, no evil shall befall you, nor shall any plague come near your dwelling; for He shall give His angels charge over you, to keep you in all your ways. In their hands they shall bear you up, lest you dash your foot against a stone" (Psalm 91: 1-12 NKJV).

1. **Read:** As a group, read the Scripture passage aloud at least five times. If possible, use different Bible translations. Get a feel for what God is saying. Highlight key words and ideas.

2. **Question:** With what are you wrestling? Every believer in Jesus battles something like fear, anxiety, intimidation, sadness, disappointment, covetousness and lust. Share with one another.

3. **Meditate:** Spend five minutes quietly pondering, musing and chewing over the Scripture passage. Ask the Holy Spirit to give you understanding. Nobody should speak during this time.

4. **Share:** Share what insights and Scriptures the Lord brings. Keep the sharing short.

5. **Questions:** How do these insights affect your life? What lies have you believed? What truth will you now ask the Holy Spirit to put on your mind and inscribe on your heart? What does this passage of Scripture reveal about God's character and nature?

6. **Prayer**: Finish by sitting or standing in a tight circle. Ask the Holy Spirit to help you creatively turn both Psalm 91 and God's thoughts into significant prayer. Use three types of prayer:

- **Personal prayer:** Pray specifically, not generally, for each group member. What is God's mind toward Jenny, Mark or Jeanette … or whoever?
- **Declaration prayer:** As part of your praying, turn Psalm 91: 1-12 into words of declaration—declaring the Lordship of Jesus over every anxiety, worry, concern, challenge and offence.
- **Petition prayer**: You may also turn them into words of petition, asking for God's intervention in an area of concern. However He leads, be specific and keep the prayers on track. This is not the time to pray for things unrelated to the chapter or outside the group.

CHAPTER FIVE

A Transformed Life

"The nature of that holiness which the true Christian seeks to possess is no other than the restoration of the image of God to his soul."
—William Wilberforce

"I appeal to you therefore, brethren, and beg of you in view of all the mercies of God, to make a decisive dedication of your bodies—*presenting all your members and faculties*—as a living sacrifice, holy (devoted, consecrated) and well pleasing to God, which is your reasonable (rational, intelligent) service and spiritual worship. *Do not be conformed* to this world—this age, fashioned after and adapted to its external, superficial customs. *But be transformed* (changed) by the (entire) renewal of your mind—by its new ideals, and its new attitude—so that you may prove (for yourselves) what is the good and acceptable and perfect will of God, even the thing which is good and acceptable and perfect (in His sight for you)" (Romans 12: 1-2 Amplified Version, emphasis added).

In chapter four we considered the renewal of our mind by choosing and allowing the mind of Christ to become our own. (Philippians 2: 5). Now we consider the result of renewal—the glorious transformation of our lives, inside and out. Taking up our inherited position "in Christ", all is to be cleansed, redeemed and renewed—our hearts, values, attitudes, speech, behaviour, relationships and ambitions. No part is left untouched. We are to experience the joy of being re-parented by our heavenly Father, developing godly character and learning the way of the cross.

In Christ

Transformation takes place because we are now "in Christ Jesus". We hold a new and privileged position, seated in heavenly places in Him (Ephesians 2: 6). He was raised to triumph, and so, too, we have been raised to rule and reign in life (Ephesians 1: 15 - 2: 10). This magnificent truth absolutely transforms our mindset and the way we live life. We are no longer earthbound in our heart and thinking, groveling in the dust. We now think as those who are above, not below, over, not under, farsighted, not shortsighted. We are in Christ Jesus "far above all principalities and power and might and dominion,

and every name that is named, not only in this age but also in that which is to come". If all things are under Jesus' feet, they are under ours as well (Ephesians 1: 21-23 NKJV). Now that is radical change!

Paul also says that because of our new position in Christ, "every spiritual blessing" in Christ Jesus is ours. Note these are the spiritual blessings he refers to—in Christ Jesus we are chosen, blameless (Ephesians 1: 4), adopted, accepted (Ephesians 1: 5-6), redeemed, forgiven, predestined to obtain an inheritance and sealed with the Holy Spirit of promise to guarantee it (Ephesians 1: 7, 11, 13). What an amazing transformation from where we used to be—distant, orphaned, accused, lost, unforgiven, unhealed and vulnerable. In Christ Jesus, everything is new and is being made new! Nothing in our lives, past, present or future, need be left untouched by God; He desires to redeem it all. He dispenses healing, spiritual sight, abundant life, mental and emotional freedom—from darkness to light, and releases daily doses of strength and overcoming power.

> "Jesus said, "The Spirit of the LORD is upon Me, because He has anointed Me to preach the gospel to the poor; He has sent Me to heal the broken-hearted, to proclaim liberty to the captives and recovery of sight to the blind, to set at liberty those who are oppressed; to proclaim the acceptable year of the LORD"" (Luke 4: 18-19 NKJV).

At the Cross

Radical change takes place in the heart, not the physical organ, but in the core of our being. The most frequently used Biblical term for man's inner nature or character is "heart"; it is used 823 times in our English Bible. It is interesting to note that in the Old Testament, the word for "heart" and "mind" is the same word—"Lev or Levav". We think (mind), decide (will) and feel (emotions) in our heart.

It is because of God's mercy that He continues to reveal sin lodged in our mind, will and emotions so that we can confess it, repent and walk in the new freedom purchased by the blood of Jesus shed on the cross. However, the cross is not just about the redemption of sin; Jesus also took upon Himself our suffering and pain. He is our sin-bearer *and pain-bearer*. We are a broken people and we are to lay past and present emotional pain, grief, loss and failure upon Him at the cross. Far from condemning our weaknesses, wounds and faults, He validates their reality by being the Pain-bearer. What a relief it is to be healed, restored and forgiven; none of us were perfect when we entered the kingdom of God. We are graciously cleaned up by God as we submit to His process of renewal, allowing Him to remove the weights that have held us back, and to teach us how to walk in the victory and power of the Holy Spirit.

> "All we like sheep have gone astray; we have turned, every one, to his own way; and the LORD has laid on Him *the iniquity* (Hebrew: "Avon"—evil, fault, sin, guilt, blame, moral illness, perversion, crookedness, and punishment of iniquity) of us all" (Isaiah 53: 6, NKJV, emphasis added).

Iniquities are the sinful tendencies we are born with, which direct the course of our lives. It is more than sin or transgression; it is our own evil bent—our propensity to engage in particular sins, which we inherited from our ancestors. A tremendous change takes place when we lay our iniquities upon Jesus; we break free from our inherited past.

> "Jesus said, "*If* you *abide in My word*, you are My disciples indeed. And you shall know the truth, *and the truth shall make you free*"" (John 8: 31-32 NKJV, emphasis added)

Do note the word, "if"; becoming free and remaining free is conditional upon abiding in the Word. It is the "abiding Word", which sets us free from the inside out. The consequences of not teaching believers that the Holy Spirit, through the abiding Word of God, should transform them are serious:

1. Believers remain deeply affected and controlled by inherited evil tendencies.
2. They still carry past wounds, grief, loss and failure, instead of being set free and healed.

Face to Face with God

As much as we would like everything to be instantaneous and automatic, growing in Christ-likeness is not like that. It is the consequence of living in the presence of God. It takes devotion, commitment, time, effort and diligence on our part. Face to face with God, our Father, in the light of His eternal Word and infused with the power of the Holy Spirit, we become like them. Biblical meditation fine-tunes all our senses to know who God is, and what His presence can accomplish in us.

> "But we all, with unveiled face, beholding as in a mirror the glory of the Lord, are being transformed into the same image from glory to glory, just as by the Spirit of the Lord" (2 Corinthians 3: 18 NKJV).

> "The thief does not come except to steal, and to kill, and to destroy. I have come that they may have life, and that they may have it more abundantly" (John 10: 10 NKJV).

> "I have come as a light into the world, that whoever believes in Me should not abide in darkness" (John 12: 46 NKJV).

Walk Worthy of the Lord

Having explained our new position in Christ Jesus and the glorious nature of the transformation offered, Paul describes in Ephesians the implications and responsibilities which accompany transformation. Transformation is much more than a nice feeling or personal blessing! We are to "walk worthy of the calling" (Ephesians 4: 1), "keep the unity of the Spirit in the bond of peace" (4: 3), "equip and edify the Body of Christ" (4: 12) "grow up" (4: 15) "put off" the old life and "put on" the new (4: 17-24).

> "This I say, therefore, and testify in the Lord, that you should no longer walk as the rest of the Gentiles walk, in the futility of their mind, having their understanding darkened, being alienated from the life of God, because of the ignorance that is in them, because of the blindness of their heart; who, being past feeling, have given themselves over to lewdness, to work all uncleanness with greediness. But you have not so learned Christ, if indeed you have heard Him and have been taught by Him, as the truth is in Jesus: that you put off, concerning your former conduct, the old man which grows corrupt according to the deceitful lusts, and be renewed in the spirit of your mind, and that you put on the new man which was created according to God, in true righteousness and holiness" (Ephesians 4: 17-24 NKJV).

Transformation means that we honour the Lord, live in unity, grow in spiritual maturity and are proactive in maintaining openness and accountability in relationships. We will champion godliness and refuse ground to Satan. Listen to King David:

> "How can a young man cleanse his way? By taking heed according to Your word. With my whole heart I have sought You; O, let me not wander from Your commandments! Your word I have hidden in my

heart that I might not sin against You. Blessed are
You, O LORD! Teach me Your statutes" (Psalm 119:
9-12 NKJV).

"Keep your heart with all diligence, for out of it
spring the issues of life. Put away from you a deceitful
mouth, and put perverse lips far from you. Let your
eyes look straight ahead, and your eyelids look right
before you. Ponder the path of your feet, and let all
your ways be established. Do not turn to the right or
the left; remove your foot from evil" (Proverbs 4: 23-
27 NKJV).

A Pure Heart

"Who may ascend into the hill of the LORD? Or who
may stand in His holy place? *He who has clean hands and
a pure heart*, who has not lifted up his soul to an idol,
nor sworn deceitfully. He shall receive blessing from
the LORD" (Psalm 24: 3-5 NKJV, emphasis added).

Transformation includes getting rid of impurities. The Greek word
for "pure" is "katheros" is used 27 times in the New Testament.
Fundamentally, it means that which is clean, or free from
contaminating substances (cf. Danker Greek-English Lexicon of the
NT). Our hearts are to be clean, free from the impurity of sin, evil
motive, sickness and evil spirits. Jesus taught: "Blessed are the pure in
heart for they shall see God" (Matthew 5: 8). It could be translated,
"Blessed, happy and fortunate are those who have the dross of their
heart skimmed off in the searing white heat of life's crucible, for in
doing so they experience the holiness of God".

Gold, boiled in a cast iron pot, brings the impurities to the
top. Skimmed off, the pure liquid gold remains. A pure heart is pure

because it has yielded to the refining process—it has said, "Yes" to the sanctifying work of the Holy Spirit. It is not a process designed to harm, it is God's process for preparing the bride of Christ for His return. Tests and trials prove our faith in God, and none is exempt. We are being refined and prepared for the Bridegroom!

> "In this you greatly rejoice, though now for a little while, if need be, you have been grieved by various trials, that the genuineness of your faith, being much more precious than gold that perishes, though it is tested by fire, may be found to praise, honour, and glory at the revelation of Jesus Christ, whom having not seen you love. Though now you do not see Him, yet believing, you rejoice with joy inexpressible and full of glory, receiving the end of your faith—the salvation of your souls" (1 Peter 1: 6-9 NKJV).

The heart of man is contaminated and polluted by sin and the world, and the extent of the pollution is clearly seen in what is going on in the world—genocide, corruption, stealing, deceit, lies, covetousness, idolatry and lawlessness, from the highest levels of government to the common man on the street.

The Bible tells us that the human heart is deceitful above all things, and is desperately wicked because man is a fallen creature, subject to sin (Jeremiah 17: 9-10). Just as harmful toxins accumulate in the body causing disease, the toxin of sin ruins and contaminates the heart. This contamination hinders and resists transformation. Jesus reminds us:

> "What comes out of a man defiles a man. For from within, out of the heart of men, proceed evil thoughts, adulteries, fornications, murders, thefts, covetousness, wickedness, deceit, lewdness, an evil

eye, blasphemy, pride, foolishness. All these evil things come from within and defile a man" (Mark 7: 20-23 NKJV).

What about believers, are their hearts impure? Sadly, church splits are evidence of impurity, as are adultery, inappropriate sexual alliances, rivalries, covetousness, worldliness and pride. Our flesh will always tend towards selfish attitudes, crooked values, unseemly behaviour patterns, questionable motives, inappropriate affections, carnal desires, and egotistic dreams and thoughts. We have power and authority to resist temptation and to live entirely different.

Loving God means obeying the commands *"don't be conformed and be transformed"*. It is our willingness to be transformed which reveals we love Him with all our heart (our very being), all our soul and with our entire mind. There does not appear to be too much wriggle-room for negotiation, does there? God commands whole-hearted commitment, because He longs for intimacy with us, without barrier or restraint. He wants close family relationships, unhindered by sin.

> "Jesus said to him, 'You shall love the LORD your God with all your heart, with all your soul, and with your entire mind.' This is the first and great commandment. In addition, the second is like it: 'You shall love your neighbour as yourself.' On these two commandments hang all the Law and the Prophets" (Matthew 22: 37-40 NKJV).

A True Story of Transformation: Alice

We hosted a Mission Encouragement Trust retreat for single missionaries in Africa. The theme, "Come, now is the time to worship", was based on the pattern of the tabernacle of Moses

(Exodus 25). Therefore, the meeting hall was set up to replicate the tabernacle. Over a period of seven days, we expounded the Cross by means of the rich symbolism of the Gate, the Altar of Sacrifice, the Laver of Washing, the Menorah, the Table of Showbread, the Altar of Incense and the Ark of the Covenant.

Alice, a missionary in Africa, came to that retreat. It was immediately apparent, as she arrived at the retreat centre, that she was a deeply troubled person. Her overtly coarse, loud and sarcastic humour, self-seeking and disruptive behaviour and inappropriate dress sent shockwaves through the retreat community. This girl oozed trouble. What were we, as MET retreat staff, to do about Alice? The Lord seemed to say, accept, love and pray for her. Beneath the troublesome exterior was a deeply hurt and wounded soul. As the retreat progressed, Alice remained challenging and aggressive in all situations, and we were at our wits' end. It was one thing for Alice to choose to behave in that manner, but it was sad to see and hear how she was affecting the other participants. The earnest prayer vigil continued. Only God could break through in Alice's life and, in the meantime, we had to trust Him to handle the fallout.

On the last day, we shared communion in the Holy Place— the place of the Menorah (light), the Table of Showbread (Word and fellowship) and the Altar of Incense (prayer). A beautiful atmosphere filled the meeting hall; God was there walking among His people. Alice sat staring into space; her sparse dress seemed provocative set against the purity of the moment. As communion commenced, Jan, led by the Spirit broke bread with her. There was no desire to do so; Alice's behaviour had taken its toll.

"Alice, this is the Body of Christ broken for you".

Full of shame, Alice looked up into Jan's eyes and broke the matzo bread. As the bread snapped in two, she involuntarily fell to the floor writhing in pain and torment. We covered her with loving ministry. Her screams and tears were agonising; God was meeting with her. Swiftly, we gathered everyone to pray. In the name of Jesus, demons were addressed and commanded to flee. Alice looked as though she was out cold, but then unexpectedly her body would shudder with more twisting, struggling, tears and pain. This went on for some time, as did the concerted prayer and impromptu worship. All of a sudden, as the holy presence of God descended, her countenance was serene and calm; it was as if the sun had risen in her soul. During the night we spent time with Alice, hearing her confession and allowing deep and infected wounds to be opened up for cleansing. God was doing a work of grace by His Word and the Spirit.

The following morning, during corporate worship, Alice walked purposefully to the front of the meeting. She was dressed beautifully and appropriately in white. The glory of God shone on her face.

"Jan, may I have the microphone? May I say something?"

As Jan passed the microphone, we all held our breath.

"I didn't really want to come to this retreat. I knew from the information that it would be spiritual and I was tired of false spirituality of leaders. I have felt used, abused, and have stored up anger and bitterness. I know I have been deliberately difficult at this retreat, and have taken out my pain on the leaders. Mintie and Jan, I ask your forgiveness. I am so sorry for what I have put you and your staff through. I deliberately provoked you to see if you were like the others who had hurt me. Your love, graciousness and acceptance in the face of my disruption and aggression melted my hardened heart." You could hear a pin drop. She continued, "I also ask the forgiveness of everyone here. Last night during communion, I was set free from years of hurt and pain. God's love broke in, revealing to my heart that I am precious and special, and that He will never leave nor forsake me. I still have some things to sort out. I need to go to leaders and ask their forgiveness and make things right and I will make sure I do. This week at the cross challenged and changed my life."

We met Alice a few years later in London. God had truly transformed her life!

Prayer

Lord, change my heart. Convict me of sin. Uncover unrighteousness and unhealed wounds from my past, and in Your mercy lead me to repentance and healing. Fill me with the Holy Spirit and open Your Word to my heart. Teach me how to walk in the Spirit. Amen.

- Having prayed this prayer, spend time waiting on the Lord.
- Open your heart for examination.
- Be willing to make confession and repent before the Lord.
- If things surface which are too difficult for you to deal with alone, ask a trusted friend to hear your confession and pray with you. The more transparent we are with God and others, the deeper God can work.
- Be prepared to go and ask forgiveness of one you have hurt or offended.
- Be prepared to make reparation if you have stolen what belongs to another.
- Be thorough and specific in repentance.

- Be profuse in praise and thanksgiving for God's redemption.

Preparation for Life Group

"Finally, brethren, whatever things are true, whatever things are noble, whatever things are just, whatever things are pure, whatever things are lovely, whatever things are of good report, if there is any virtue and if there is anything praiseworthy—*meditate on these things.* The things which you learned and received and heard and saw in me, these do, and the God of peace will be with you" (Philippians 4: 8-9 NKJV, emphasis added).

Meditate on Philippians 4: 8-9; then take time to consider and answer the following questions. Write down your answers.

From the Bible and your own experience:

- What "*things*" do you know to be true about God?
- What is noble about God?
- How does God act justly?
- What do you understand about the purity of God?
- How have you experienced the loveliness of God?
- What good report do you have about God?
- What do you perceive as virtuous and praiseworthy about God?
- What was the result of meditating on the virtues and character of God?

Give thanks and praise to the Lord—this is our God. These are His virtues.

- Which godly virtues and godly characteristics has God developed in your life? What have you "learned, received, heard and seen" in your walk with God? Prepare a short personal testimony to share with the Life Group (no more than 7 minutes).

Life Group

- Spend 15 minutes sharing on your meditation upon Philippians 4: 8-9.
- Share the prepared testimonies (7 minutes or less). What have you "*learned, received, heard and seen*" about God in your spiritual walk? Which parts of God's character have been developed in you, and how?
- Pray for each one as they finish sharing. Be sensitive to feelings of vulnerability.
- Discuss how you can help each other to stay committed to the process of transformation.

CHAPTER SIX

The Engrafted Word

"One thing I have noticed in studying the Word of God, and that is, when a man is filled with the Spirit he deals largely with the Word of God, whereas the man who is filled with his own ideas refers rarely to the Word of God. He gets along without it, and you seldom see it mentioned in his discourses." —D L Moody

"Therefore lay aside all filthiness and overflow of wickedness, and *receive with meekness the implanted word, which is able to save your souls*. But be doers of the word and not hearers only, deceiving yourselves. For if anyone is a hearer of the word and not a doer, he is like a man observing his natural face in a mirror; for he observes himself, goes away, and immediately forgets what kind of man he was. But he who looks into the perfect law of liberty and continues in it, and is not a forgetful hearer but a doer of the work, this one will be blessed in what he does" (James 1: 21-25, NKJV, emphasis added).

In James 1: 21 the Bible is called *"the engrafted Word."* The Greek word rendered here as "engrafted", and indeed the English word *engrafted*, has the meaning of "*planting into*". Hence the word has sometimes been rendered implanted—"*the implanted Word*" *(NIV)*. However, what does it mean to be "engrafted" or "to graft" something?

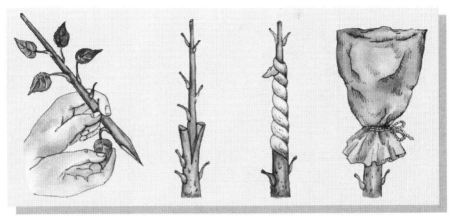

Grafting begins with a wild root-stock. You take a cutting from another plant species and graft it into the root-stock. A cut—an incision, is made to split the wild root stock to receive the new shoot. The two tightly bound in a living union form a completely new plant. It is no longer a wild plant, but has taken on the nature of the plant grafted into it.

This is yet another beautiful analogy of how the Word enters our hearts to bring sanctification to our souls (mind, will and emotions). Often it is during tough times when we are vulnerable and wounded, that God is able to make an incision in our tender hearts to engraft a new shoot of His life-giving Word. God engrafts, and we absorb words of comfort, consolation, encouragement and correction, which change us to become more like Him, forming Christ within. The fruit produced from every engrafting is not according to the "nature" of the original stock (our old nature/our flesh), but according to the nature of the new graft—Christ Jesus (Galatians 5: 22). There is great reward in engrafting every single verse in the Bible, because "*all scripture is given by inspiration of God, and is profitable for doctrine, for reproof, for correction, for instruction in righteousness"* (2 Timothy 3: 16 NKJV, emphasis added). Jesus said:

> *"I have given them Your word*; and the world has hated them because *they are not of the world*, just as I am not of the world. I do not pray that You should take them out of the world, but that You should keep them from the evil one. They are not of the world, just as I am not of the world. Sanctify them (separate to Me) by Your truth. Your word is truth. As You sent Me into the world, I also have sent them into the world. And for their sakes I sanctify Myself, that they also may be sanctified by the truth" (John 17: 14-19, NKJV, emphasis added).

Receive with Meekness

We must therefore submit ourselves to the Word of God, as the wild root-stock submits to the process of engrafting—with meekness. Considering the context of this verse, the best and most simple definition of meekness is "a teachable attitude, submissiveness, freedom from haughty self-sufficiency, tender of spirit, and gentle". With this definition, James 1: 21 would read, "...*receive the engrafted word humbly and submissively, with a teachable and tender attitude* ..." The wild root-stock demonstrates meekness as it loses its old "wild" life to receive an implant which produces new life with new fruit; it gives up what it was, to become what the new shoot would make it—a new plant.

In the Old Covenant God wrote His Law/Word on tablets of stone, but now in the New Covenant, cut in the blood of Jesus, He writes His Law/Word into the flesh of human hearts, by the Holy Spirit. This is not shallow or superficial; the Holy Spirit cuts into the flesh to make the Word one with that heart.

"Behold, the days are coming, says the LORD, when I will make a new covenant with the house of Israel and with the house of Judah—not according to the covenant that I made with their fathers in the day that I took them by the hand to lead them out of the land of Egypt, My covenant which they broke, though I was a husband to them, says the LORD. But this is the covenant that I will make with the house of Israel after those days, says the LORD: *I will put My law in their minds, and write it on their hearts; and I will be their God, and they shall be My people.* No more shall every man teach his neighbour, and every man his brother, saying, 'Know the LORD,' for they all shall know Me, from the least of them to the greatest of them, says the LORD. For I will forgive their iniquity, and their sin I will remember no more" (Jeremiah 31: 31-34, NKJV, emphasis added).

"These things I have spoken to you while being present with you. But the Helper, the Holy Spirit, whom the Father will send in My name, He will teach you all things, and bring to your remembrance all things that I said to you" (John 14: 25-27 NKJV).

We are not able to receive God's Word with a "know-it-all" attitude or an "I-don't-need-this" attitude, or indeed, with an "I-refuse-to-change" attitude. When we are high-minded and full of pride, all we take note of are our own opinions. We think we have arrived and there is nothing more to be learned. We have placed ourselves, our interests and desires above God's. The moment we are arrogant and proud, our hearts and minds become unteachable and our chosen loftiness denies entrance to God's Word. In this condition, we are in grave danger of dying spiritually as a result of spiritual starvation.

Engrafting Through Biblical Meditation

Biblical meditation requires a teachable attitude. A meek person realises that, no matter how many facts he knows, no matter how many times a passage has been studied, there is always more that God delights in revealing. There is always more wisdom and knowledge to be received, and much more transformation of heart which needs to occur. With an attitude of meekness we are open to hear about our sin and shortcomings and we patiently and thankfully, desire to be transformed into the likeness of Jesus. Therefore, hearing the Word only is not enough; our lives must show that the engrafted Word has taken root by the way we act upon it. We must be "doers of the Word" (James 1: 22-25). John says,

> "For I rejoiced greatly when brethren came and testified of the truth that is in you, just as you walk in the truth. I have no greater joy than to hear that my children walk in truth" (3 John 3: 3–4 NKJV).

Believers are not exempt from tests and trials, for example, chronic illness, bereavement, cancer, heart attacks, emotional breakdown, thefts, accidents, messy divorces, relational conflicts or redundancy. Shaken, the fallout is often worse than the event itself. There is loss on all fronts—loss of independence, loss of financial stability, loss of warmth, comfort and love, loss of ministry, loss of reputation, loss of longstanding friendships and the loss of any sense of permanence. Every loss creates need and emotional turmoil. It may feel as though a tornado has ripped through our lives and it takes a huge effort to clear up the debris and start the rebuilding process.

In the life of a believer, the severity of any storm tests the depth of the Word deposited in us and gives opportunity for God to do a deeper work of grace. At the close of the "Sermon on the Mount" (Matthew 5-7) Jesus explains the stark contrast between a person who receives the engrafted Word with meekness and acts on it, and one who does not.

> "Therefore whoever hears these sayings of Mine, and does them, I will liken him to a wise man who built his house on the rock: and the rain descended, the floods came, and the winds blew and beat on that house; and it did not fall, for it was founded on the rock. But everyone who hears these sayings of Mine, and does not do them, will be like a foolish man who built his house on the sand: and the rain descended, the floods came, and the winds blew and beat on that house; and it fell. And great was its fall" (Matthew 7: 24-27 NKJV).

When our backs are against the wall, is there rock or sand beneath our feet? Do we stand or fall? God engrafts His Word into our hearts so that we may stand strong in the day of trouble.

Asaph's Psalm

Let's read Asaph's psalm—Psalm 77:

> "I cried out to God with my voice—to God with my voice; and He gave ear to me. In the day of my trouble I sought the Lord; my hand was stretched out in the night without ceasing; my soul refused to be comforted. I remembered God, and was troubled; I complained, and my spirit was overwhelmed. Selah

> You hold my eyelids open; I am so troubled that I cannot speak. *I have considered* the days of old, the years of ancient times. *I call to remembrance* my song in the night; *I meditate within my heart, and my spirit makes diligent search.*

Will the Lord cast off forever? And will He be favourable no more? Has His mercy ceased forever? Has His promise failed forevermore? Has God forgotten to be gracious? Has He in anger shut up His tender mercies? Selah

And I said, *"This is my anguish; but I will remember* the years of the right hand of the Most High." *I will remember* the works of the LORD; surely *I will remember* Your wonders of old. *I will also meditate* on all Your work, *and talk of* Your deeds. Your way, O God, is in the sanctuary; who is so great a God as our God? *You are* the God who does wonders; *You have* declared Your strength among the peoples. *You have* with Your arm redeemed Your people, the sons of Jacob and Joseph. Selah

The waters saw You, O God; the waters saw You, they were afraid; the depths also trembled. The clouds poured out water; the skies sent out a sound; *Your* arrows also flashed about. The voice of *Your* thunder was in the whirlwind; the lightning lit up the world; the earth trembled and shook. *Your way* was in the sea, *Your path* in the great waters, and *Your footsteps* were not known. *You led Your people like a flock* by the hand of Moses and Aaron" (NKJV emphasis added).

In the midst of immense trouble, Asaph remembered the "old days" of glory and recalled songs of worship, which God had given. As the rhetorical questions spill from his mouth, he meditates upon God with intent. "Will the Lord cast off forever? And will He be favourable no more? Has His mercy ceased forever? Has His promise failed forevermore? Has God forgotten to be gracious? Has He in anger shut up His tender mercies?" Thinking of God's works, His wonders and His deeds in bygone days, he remembers how every question of life concerning God's people could only find resolution in the presence of God—in the sanctuary. As inner contemplation quickly moves on to vocal declaration (Romans 10: 17), he listens to his own voice extolling God's wonders and strength. His testimony strengthens his heart. He had the testimony of God's works deeply rooted in him. He was assured that there was nothing to fear; God had always led Israel like the shepherd of a flock and He would not stop caring for His sheep.

What was Asaph doing? He was refocusing. Fixing his eyes on God, he gained God's perspective. He meditated (remembered, recalled, declared) on God. He literally dug deep into what He knew of God, His power and His ways. Asaph's spiritual storehouse was full, his reserves abundant.

> *"The entrance of Your words* gives light; it gives understanding to the simple. I opened my mouth and panted, for I longed for Your commandments. Look upon me and be merciful to me, as Your custom is toward those who love Your name. Direct my steps by Your word, and let no iniquity have dominion over me" (Psalm 119: 130-133, NKJV, emphasis added).

Preparation for Meditation

The following steps, taken from Appendix 2—"A Guide to Meditating upon the Word of God", will help prepare the way for God to engraft His Word. They are simple steps, which we will practice alone and in Life Group during the remaining weeks of our discipleship study.

1. **Place:**
   Find and designate the space where you will be alone with God. You have a divine appointment.

2. **Switch off:**

   Switch *off* your mobile telephone. You are not available.

3. **Settle down:**

   Find a comfortable position, close your eyes and breathe deeply.

4. **Turn toward God:**

   Lift your face and incline your heart toward God. Let your physical body lean back, raise your hands and hold that position for two minutes.

5. **Thankfulness:**

   "Thank you, Lord Jesus, for being here". Repeat this phrase several times. You are becoming conscious of God's presence. Linger a while.

6. **Open your Bible to Psalm 92:**

   This is a psalm which gives great hope in the midst of a trial. Trials present opportunity for spiritual growth. However, what will that growth look like?

   • Lay your hand on the text and thank the Lord for His precious Word. As you do so ask Him to engraft Psalm 92 into your heart. Remember, meditation is not only upon words, phrases or imagery, it is upon God.

   • Thank Him that His divine Word has power over every work of the enemy. Thank Him that He desires to speak to you. Thank Him for the insight He will bring.

7. **Ask:**

   Ask the Holy Spirit to lead you in this meditation as you sit quietly before the Lord.

Invite God to Engraft Psalm 92

1. Read:
Read Psalm 92 three times.

Do the fourth reading aloud. Centre your meditation specifically on verses 12-15, so take particular note when you reach those verses.

2. Wait:
- Sit quietly before the Lord and ask the Holy Spirit to speak to you through this wonderful Psalm.
- Drink in His presence as you now concentrate on verses 12-15. Read the passage again. To help facilitate this part of the exercise, Psalm 92: 12-15 has been printed in the book below.
- Write down in your notebook the first thoughts which stir in your mind.
- Underline words which stand out.

> "The righteous shall flourish like a palm tree; he shall grow like a cedar in Lebanon. Those who are planted in the house of the LORD shall flourish in the courts of our God. They shall still bear fruit in old age; they shall be fresh and flourishing, to declare that the LORD is upright; He is my rock, and there is no unrighteousness in Him" (Psalm 92: 12-15 NKJV).

3. Consider who, what, why, when, how?
Read this beautiful Psalm aloud at least four more times. Read slowly, considering each word. Pause and pray: "Holy Spirit, teach me what this passage of Scripture says".

- Now read it again. Allow different words or ideas to touch your spirit.

- o   What are the features of the palm tree and the cedar?
- o   How does a palm tree grow and flourish?
- o   To whom is growth guaranteed?
- o   What does it mean to be planted?
- o   What are the conditions for growth?
- o   How do your answers relate to your life and circumstances?

- Consider the line, "They shall still bear fruit in old age; they shall be fresh and flourishing".
  - o   What does "fresh and flourishing" mean?
  - o   What characteristics would be displayed?
  - o   What kind of fruit?
  - o   What is the result of fruitfulness?

4.   The Character of God

- What does this Psalm reveal about the character of God?

Applying Psalm 92

1.   New title:

- Give this Psalm your own title. What would you call it and why?

2.   Rewrite:

- Rewrite Psalm 92: 12-15 in your own words.
- What is God saying to you personally?

3.   Compose a prayer:

- Write a prayer which reflects the heart of the Psalm.

4.   Pray the Scripture:

- Declare/speak out your prayer to the Lord.

5. **Sing the Scripture:**
   - Put the words of verses 12-15 to a melody. Sing a new song! Even if it is a song on one note, let your spirit sing the Word!

6. **Give thanks:**
   - Give thanks for the time you have enjoyed with the Lord.
   - Once again express your desire that the truth of these verses become engrafted into your heart.

7. **Share your meditation:**
   - During the coming week return to the verses of meditation.
   - Ask the Holy Spirit to increase your understanding.

Prepare to share in the Life Group what God has revealed to you during your time of meditation.

Prayer

Lord, examine my heart for any traces of filth and wickedness. Show me any areas of pride that forbid entrance of Your Word into my heart. Implant truth day by day; I long for your Word to be established in my mind and heart. Show me how to act on the Word; to be a "doer of the Word", not just a hearer. Amen.

Life Group

- Allow each Life Group member to give feedback on his/her meditation on Psalm 92.
- Share areas of need arising from the meditation.
- Pray for one another.

CHAPTER SEVEN

Guided by God's Word

"Generally speaking, it is correct to say that the will of God for the people of God is in the Word of God." —John Stott, Anglican Clergyman and Biblical scholar

We need the guidance of God and we are utterly dependent upon Him to show, teach and lead us in His paths. As disciples of Jesus, we no longer live our way, we are committed to live His way. We are to serve Him and His purposes. The difficulty is finding out what He requires. David prayed:

> "Show me Your ways, O LORD; teach me Your paths. Lead me in Your truth and teach me, for You are the God of my salvation; on You I wait all the day" (Psalm 25: 4-5 NKJV)

- What is on His heart for the world? We tend to make guidance very personal but let's remember that much of what God would share concerns the fulfilment of His eternal plan of salvation for the world.

- Are we at a crossroads where we do not know which way to choose?

- Do we need God's wisdom for a particular decision—job, university course, life-partner, opportunity to serve at church?

- Do we need counsel in regard to a difficult relationship?
- What does God desire for the way we live our lives?

We can receive a Biblical answer to every question, need or problem. God does not expect us to know the answers, but He does expect us to ask Him (Psalm 65: 9; Proverbs 2: 10; Proverbs 27: 22). He knows we *do not* have wisdom for life. We *do not* know how to respond in a given situation. The good news is that Biblical meditation primes our hearts to hear His response; *when we ask Him* He will give wisdom, clues, insights and answers (James 1: 5).

What Now Lord?

We have stood at many types of crossroads in our personal and ministerial lives and haven't known which road to take. We needed to hear but one voice—the voice of the Lord.

- Seasons came to an end—"Lord, we sense the anointing for this season has ebbed away. What are You saying, what do You require? Which way do we go?"
- New seasons started—"Lord, where are we to base ourselves? With whom should we co-operate? How do we raise funds for the work?"
- Conflicts arose—"Give us discernment to know what is going on. Show us what in our hearts is creating difficulty. How should we respond to accusations? Is this breakdown in work relationships ours to sort out at this time?"

- Many missionaries needed support and care—"Lord, to whom are You sending us? Where do You want us to go?"

- Many times we did not know the missionaries we came alongside on the mission field or at the retreats for single missionaries which we hosted—"Lord, You know these dear people, what should we take with us? How should we prepare? Which word of encouragement do You have for them? How should we structure this retreat? Which staff should we bring in to help?"

- We faced dangers as we travelled—"Lord, what do we do now? Which way?"

- Disasters struck—"Lord, where should we go for help?"

- The opportunity of marriage turned up unexpectedly for Jan—"Lord, are You in this? Is this Your chosen one? What about our partnership in ministry? Should the ministry continue?"

Biblical meditation unlocked our minds and hearts to understanding God, His ways and His plans. Just as Jesus was totally tuned to the voice of His Father to do His will, so we must be too.

Jesus said:

> "My food is to do the will of Him who sent Me, and to finish His work" (John 4: 34-35 NKJV).

> "It is written, 'Man shall not live by bread alone, but by every word that proceeds from the mouth of God'" (Matthew 4: 4 NKJV).

Relational Guidance

We are often guilty of thinking of guidance narrowly, as needed only in "important" decisions to be made; for example, in an emergency, or when planning a move from A to B. The rest of the time, we just work things out for ourselves. However, God does not think like that; He does not just dish out good ideas on request. He thinks and guides relationally.

A casual online visit to "MapQuest" can give us directions from Brighton to Glasgow, but checking for directions does not establish a relationship with the writer of the map programme. Do we casually "Google" God in the same way? Are we guilty of treating God like an information bureau? Presenting prayer requests to the Lord does not necessarily indicate a depth of relationship. Whilst we may be genuinely interested in getting answers to questions like, "Should I serve God in Africa or Asia?", "Which university should I go to?" or "Shall I marry this man/woman?" Perhaps a better relational question is, "Lord, which decision will draw me closer to You?" It reveals a heart which first honours relationship with Him. The Bible provides guidance for life situations, but knowing that will not help us at all if we are fickle with our Guide!

God guides in the context of an intimate and loving relationship. He wants the best and takes primary responsibility for our care as we step out on the way He chooses. God guides with a close eye on our health and well-being.

The Fear of the Lord

The Bible says that God reveals His ways to those who fear Him. (Psalm 25: 14) In other words, He shares what is on His heart in the context of consecration, honour, reverence and respect. When the reverential fear of the Lord is present, our heavenly Father can entrust what is on His heart. He knows it will be cherished, revered and acted upon in a way which glorifies Him. This is not a fear where we recoil or stand at a distance; it is a holy fear which respects and honours God as God. It is a deep and committed love, which wants to please and never offend Him.

Since the fear of the Lord is the beginning of wisdom, we are promised that we will know how to act, what to do, where to go and how to respond. The absence of the fear of the Lord creates a permissive society where people only live to please themselves. They live in confusion and without restraint.

- It is the fear of the Lord which produces obedience; it respects the authority of the Word of God (Psalm 111: 10). We don't need any further guidance from God when it is clear in His Word. The only decision to be made is whether we will be obedient or disobedient to what He has said, and there are consequences of both.
- It is the fear of the Lord which keeps us from sinning. When we face temptation the fear of the Lord woven into the fabric of our heart says, "No!" (Exodus 20: 20).
- The fear of the Lord faithfully steers our lives. It guides us about what to avoid and where not to go! It keeps us on track to complete the tasks God has appointed (Hebrews 11: 7). Noah didn't just start, he finished! Godly fear acted as a guide saying, "press on, press on, press on!" The absence of the fear of the Lord means we decide what we will do and when we will do it. We are driven by selfish ambition, not led by the Holy Spirit.
- The fear of the Lord avoids evil and is health to our body and strength to our bones. It keeps us healthy, because we stop ingesting junk and filth (Proverbs 3: 7-8).
- Proverbs 19: 23 tells us that, "The fear of the LORD leads to life, and he who has it will abide in satisfaction; He will not be visited by evil." (NKJV)

In all your Ways Acknowledge Him

There is nothing hidden or complicated about receiving God's guidance; it occurs supernaturally - naturally, as we walk with Him in reverential fear. God delights in showing us the way. Proverbs 3: 5-6 sums it up this way, "Trust in the Lord with all your heart, and lean not on your own understanding; *in all your ways acknowledge* Him, and *He shall* direct your paths" (NKJV emphasis added).

The word, "ways" ("derech" in Hebrew) means "a road, a course of human conduct, the manner of life which one lives, or a mode of action". It suggests sharing with Him all the details of our lives—our plans, hopes, and concerns. The word, "acknowledge" ("Yada" in Hebrew) means to know intimately by observation, investigation, reflection, or firsthand experience. This verse describes a relationship of intimate discovery where everything is mutually shared. It is far removed from thinking that somehow God hides His will where we cannot find it, or, that guidance is a matter of letting our Bible drop open with a pin in our hand. Guidance is "known" as we "know" the Guide. It is simple, intimacy with God and His Word leads us to know the heart of God. We are guided by His very presence. Therefore, there is not a day or a moment, relationship or situation, where we will not be steered on a "road, course or mode of action" if we live intimately with God.

This has such amazing synergy with Biblical meditation. To meditate on the Word (think, ponder, consider) is to relate intimately with God, face to face. As we grow in the practice of meditation, we become so familiar with God and His ways that the answers to our many questions become evident. Of the many benefits of Biblical meditation, surely the promise of intimacy with our heavenly Father, our Lord Jesus Christ and the Holy Spirit is to be prized above all other.

Relational Prayer

When seeking guidance, the combination of meditation on the Word with prayer is a necessary and potent force. Prayer is a priestly role assigned by God to the Body of Christ (1 Peter 2: 5). It is relational and Jesus placed it at the heart of Christian living. Sadly, the Church has largely neglected both its priestly function and intimacy in prayer! Prayer meetings tend to be one-way communication with many petitions, little meditation on the Scriptures and very little waiting to hear. How can we know the counsel of God without meditation on His Word? How can we hear when we do all the talking?

Praying with humility and meekness brings a realisation that it is neither *our* will, nor *our* way, but His that we seek. He is Lord and all our orders and instructions come from Him. He directs the work of the Kingdom on earth and is faithful to show us our small part.

Effective prayer unites meditation, worship, waiting on the Lord, listening to His heart and declaring His counsel. Since the Word of God is the will of God, that is where to begin. Having meditated and heard the voice of the Lord, we can be confident in petition and supplication, having assurance of answers. We need not tag "If it be Thy will" onto every petition. God's Word is His will!

What about Following our Instincts?

Should we be guided by our senses—"a gut feeling"? Of course, there is nothing wrong with using our senses, but we must make sure that our senses are regularly instructed in God's ways (Hebrews 5: 14). Even common sense remains but "common", not of God, if it is not in line with His Word!

We don't doubt that we have been "given a brain" to use, but the question still remains, is our brain renewed and aligned with the Word of God in order to be able to make sound and godly decisions?

Should we "follow our hearts"? To follow our heart is fine if our heart is washed by the Word and cleansed through repentance. If we are to follow our heart we should make sure that it is governed by the Word of God. If not, we will only be led by instincts. Is our heart filled with His way of thinking, His counsel?

To act on any level with no reference to God or His will is arrogant; it suggests we are living by our own fleshly ideas. If we actively engage with God, He promises that He will not only direct, but also watch over us. Oswald Chambers said, "Faith never knows where it is being led, but it loves and knows the One Who is leading".

"Do not be wise in your own eyes; fear the LORD and depart from evil. It will be health to your flesh and strength to your bones" (Proverbs 3: 7-8 NKJV).

"I will instruct you and teach you in the way you should go; I will counsel you and watch over you. Do not be like the horse or the mule, which have no understanding but must be controlled by bit and bridle" (Psalm 32: 8-9 NKJV).

"So then faith comes by hearing, and hearing by the word of God" (Romans 10: 17 NKJV).

How Guidance Works

For 22 years, 1992 – 2014, at the request of supporters, friends, churches and mission agencies, we pastorally visited hundreds of missionaries in their field locations. Many were feeling lonely, discouraged and disappointed in relationships and ministry; some were seeking new direction; others needed assurance that they were in the right place. As we came alongside, it was important that our "comfort, consolation and encouragement" (2 Corinthians 1: 3-4) came from God, not ourselves. Our advice and help needed to be from the Spirit and relevant to their need, offering "fresh bread"—a living Word from God, not stale morsels of the past. Therefore, each time we travelled, we spent long periods immersing ourselves in the Word of God to hear what God would say.

Biblical meditation focused our mind and heart on the Lord, energising us for the work ahead. It made us sensitive to God's voice and opened our hearts to hear His counsel and direction. Rarely was there an instantaneous "knowing" what to prepare by way of spiritual encouragement; it took time and commitment to wait on the Lord to hear. As God honed our pastoral skills, we soon learned that the greatest gift to offer another was a word of encouragement from the Scriptures, inspired by the Holy Spirit. When planning visits, we were often "in the dark" with little natural knowledge of what was ahead. Only He knew the needs and circumstances of each missionary. Only He knew the perfect time to move between mission locations. Only He knew what travel difficulties lay at and beyond the border control of each of the former communist countries. We needed guidance. Questions about timing, routes, who to visit, what to take with, practical and spiritual needs, raising funds needed to be submitted to the Lord. Repeatedly and faithfully, He guided with spine-tingling attention to detail.

Unsuitable Harbours

In 1998, we prepared for a pastoral trip to missionaries in Hungary, Romania and Poland. We travelled from place to place in the well-appointed campervan that the Lord had provided. Whilst waiting on the Lord, the Holy Spirit drew our attention to the Apostle Paul's eventful journey to Rome, recorded in Acts 27. What a rich and personally edifying study!

During the hours of reading, pondering, research, examination and prayer, several things happened. Firstly, the passage seemed to issue a warning to listen carefully to the Lord at each stage of the journey. We should be flexible with our itinerary and move as the Lord guided us. There would be a time to stay in one place, and there would be a time to move on. Secondly, as we meditated and prayed a deep love entered our heart for those we would visit, many of whom we had never met before.

Weeks later, with our campervan full of gifts and blessings, and our mind and heart full of God's Word and Spirit, we set out on a remarkable journey which would mirror Paul's own journey to Rome. We invite you to share our meditation, but as you do, ask the Holy Spirit to instruct you in divine guidance.

Meditation: Romans 1: 8-13 and Acts 27

Take some time to read both passages. As you read, have in mind the following questions:

- Who are the key players in this story?
- What are the geographical locations mentioned?

A Heart to Encourage

What was the motivation for Paul's trip to Rome? Paul already had the desire to visit the saints in Rome, but not even he could have envisaged how it would happen, or indeed, at what personal cost. He did finally reach his destination, but the journey was turbulent and full of difficulty. In addition, he arrived in Rome as a prisoner, not a free man. However, Paul knew, "that all things work together for good to those who love God, to those who are the called according to His purpose" (Romans 8: 28 NKJV).

The passage in Romans 1: 8-13 gives several insights into Paul's motivation:

- Paul had an ache in his heart; he longed to see the saints of Rome (Romans 1: 11). He had heard reports of a growing, but suffering Church.

- o Think about how suffering caused the early Church to grow.
- Paul's longing "to go" intensified as he prayed for them (Acts 27: 10).
  - o Why would that be?
- Paul submits his desire to go to Rome to the Lord and asks that He open a way for him (Acts 27: 10).
  - o What does this reveal about Paul's relationship with the Lord?
- Paul possessed God's heart. He wanted to impart some spiritual gift to make them strong in the midst of great suffering (Acts 27: 11).
  - o What does this reveal about Paul?
- Paul longed for the type of fellowship where faith is shared (Acts 27: 12).
  - o What does this reveal about Paul?

A Heart with a Purpose

The story in Acts 27 is the account of how God answered Paul's prayer to go to Rome. However, this was to be no easy journey; he had to press on through the "contrary winds" (Acts 27: 4).

1. Timing is very important! What did Paul learn about timing?

- The events of Paul's journey teach that sheltering in a place perceived to be an "unsuitable harbour" (Fair Havens, Acts 27: 8-12), is better than pressing on regardless of the will of God.
- The events also teach that the pressure of a goal (to get to Rome) can easily force a hasty and unwise decision. It says, "much time had been lost…" (Acts 27: 9), and that is often the pressure applied in decision making. However, God is never in a hurry; He leads us peacefully.

2. There were at least three other compelling voices, apart from God's.

- **The voice of the expert.** Instead of listening to Paul, who had a warning from God, the centurion followed the advice of the pilot and the owner of the ship (Acts 27: 11). This could be construed as the natural thing to do. After all, they were the experts; surely, Paul should listen to them? Experts may be well educated, have years of experience and may have good advice, but the voice of the Lord overrules man's wisdom. Flesh (the natural) always looks to flesh for counsel; a disciple of Jesus looks to the Spirit of God (the supernatural).

- **The voice of the majority.** It says, "the majority decided…. "(Acts 27: 12). They judged the situation naturally, not by the Holy Spirit. The majority can be wrong. God often spoke through a lone prophetic voice.

- **The voice of the weather.** "When a gentle southerly wind began to blow…" (Acts 27: 13). Not all "good" signs are from the Lord. How do we know if they are? When God's Word is richly deposited in our hearts through Biblical meditation, we will have the ability to discern (Hebrews 4: 12). The Word within prompts and directs.

Conclusions Drawn

Meditation is bearing good fruit! We are learning:

1. To know God's timing in a matter is crucial and on every occasion we should seek His counsel.

2. Without God's voice, every other voice or element will buffet, pressurise and lead us off course.

    a.   Have you ever launched into something which God did not ask you to do? Have you asked God's forgiveness for your presumption?

    b. In your life, what are the voices which constantly pressurise you?

3. To move on or stay is decided by God's voice.

    a.   Have you been guilty of "sheltering" (even hiding) when you should have "set sail" into something which God was calling you?

    b. Are you a "fair weather" Christian?

4. Our motivation for doing something must be for God's glory, not our own.

    a.   Have you been guilty of making a name for yourself?

    b. Have you confessed your pride and asked God's forgiveness?

5. Natural circumstances may form a part of guidance, but the bottom line is always, "What does God say?"

6. Circumstances may look a certain way, but the determining factor remains, what God has said.

7. When in doubt or lost, return to the last signpost where you were sure that you heard God speaking clearly. Check that you have fully obeyed all God said previously.

8. There is a time to learn lessons, repent, realign, readjust and move on. Being even one degree out today, can amount to being several miles off course in a few months. Our obedient actions may run totally contrary to the dictates of time, sensible advice, what the majority think, or fair weather.

9. The centurion guarding Paul soon realised that perfect timing was not determined by the weather, expert advice, the majority voice, or the pressure of time. God was saying to this shipload of people, "Stay put for a season, don't move on".

10. There is a time to sail and a time to stay in the harbour. God planned for them to harbour at Fair Havens only for a season – it was not His long-term plan. His long-term plan was to lead Paul to Rome.

11. Do not sacrifice the goal or destination for the sake of a few inconvenient months in an unsuitable harbour. Convenience does not necessarily confirm the will of God. Many times His will involves sacrifice. It did not look like it, but there was wisdom, protection, love, care, provision and perfect timing in God's instruction to stay put at Fair Havens for the winter season.

12. The Word says, "the harbour was not suitable to winter in" (Acts 27: 12). This is striking. Winter is the season of dormancy; it is probably not the time for new ventures. This quiet season is created by God to allow vegetation a time of rest. The earth prepares for vibrant growth in spring. God plans winter seasons in our lives, however, when winter is over and it is time to move on – MOVE!

A Crisis in Budapest

Finally, God had prepared us to leave for Eastern Europe. Our first stop was Budapest, Hungary. Parking our campervan at a local campsite, we took public transport to the home of long-term missionaries. What a special family with an amazing story to tell! Mum, Dad, and three young girls were working with a faith mission organisation.

They were building a large ministry house, which would be used as a base to train youth workers from Eastern Europe. It had been a tough journey of faith getting the project off the ground. As is common among many Christian volunteers, the faith in their hearts far exceeded the money in the bank! However, some money had come in, but it really was only a trickle. They experienced much opposition:

- Not all their supporters agreed with their building the house.
- The opinions of those who claimed expertise and knowledge were mostly unhelpful.
- Some were openly hostile.

However, the missionary family believed God and acted on what they believed He had told them. Contrary to the opposing voices, they bought the plot of land outside the city with the money they had and temporarily rented an apartment in the city centre.

The temporary accommodation was pokey and barely suitable for a growing family, however, it was in a safe part of town. Dad liked it very much, but Mum constantly longed for progress on the new house. She wanted to get the project moving to settle their young family in their own home. They tried to settle down in the rented apartment, but it was not long before stress levels rocketed once more. Without consultation or prior notice, their property owner put the apartment up for sale. However, when anger had simmered down, they discovered that it was advertised for sale at exactly the amount of money recently received from a donor. Surely that was God? Dad was utterly relieved, immediately seeing an opportunity to own their own place. Okay, it was not suitable, but his thoughts were driven by his responsibility to provide a secure home for his family. However, Mum only had eyes for the ministry house, which was in the process of being built. She felt that the money they had received was only for the new house. Tension filled the air.

As we sat down to drink coffee, Dad and Mum's differing views tumbled out. "Can you help us get some perspective on all this?" they anxiously asked. We were stunned, because their story expressed all the detail and tension of Acts 27! They, of course, were unaware of the meditation passage that God had given for that trip to Eastern Europe.

What an awesome moment! As we shared, the message of Acts 27 plunged straight into Dad's heart like an arrow. He spontaneously fell to his knees weeping, humble and unrestrained in repentance before God. That afternoon God's Word realigned his thinking and a new burst of faith filled his heart. He chose to lay aside natural thinking and embrace the more difficult journey of trusting God for the finances to build a ministry house. He had been in the grip of fear and his mind was in turmoil. He had wanted to please the Lord, but he also wanted to stay on the right side of his financial supporters. The many other voices offering natural counsel had sought to dominate his decision.

With fresh hope, they decided that an obedient response would be to visit their plot of land and erect a perimeter fence. This was to be a prophetic act of guarding the vision given by God and trusting Him with all their heart. They wrote out Scripture promises given by God for the house and buried them in the foundations. Some supporters were offended and stopped their support, but one key supporter remained right behind them—the God of Abraham, Isaac and Jacob Himself. The house remained under construction for four more years, and finally in 2002 it was finished. It remains a beautiful testimony to the faithfulness of God. Its construction mirrored the spiritual growth of each member of the family. Remaining obedient to God's Word in the face of an easier, more popular option, had sorely tried their faith, but they endured, overcame and grew in spiritual stature. God fulfilled every promise.

In 2012, Dad, only in his forties, tragically lost his fight with cancer and died. His mansion in heaven was ready, and it was time to go home. The three young girls are now beautiful young women; all three are married and God, in His great love, brought another man into Mum's life. They are all striding forward to fulfil the will of God for their lives. Dad has left an awesome legacy of faith and trust in God to his family.

Meditation upon the Word of God releases understanding of the will of God. The Holy Spirit enjoys taking a passage, a thought, a promise, an exhortation or correction, to teach and train us in the way we should go in life. Sometimes, what He speaks to us personally becomes guidance for someone else.

Did Paul Reach Rome?

Yes, he did, but disobedience on that ship was to prove costly. The storm struck and the captain and crew lost all control and direction (Acts 27: 15). Common to a ship trying desperately to survive a severe storm, virtually everything was thrown overboard to make it buoyant (Acts 27: 18-19). They threw their cargo of wheat into the sea and lost all hope of survival (Acts 27: 20, 38). The Word says that they moved on in the dark, with no stars or sun to navigate by for many days (Acts 27: 20). The storm showed no sign of abating; the agony and the nightmare felt as though it would go on forever. In His mercy, God speaks again (Acts 27: 21) and Paul once more demonstrates his confidence in God by exhorting the people to have courage (Acts 27: 23).

> "Last night an angel of the God whose I am and whom I serve stood beside me and said, "Do not be afraid, Paul. You must stand trial before Caesar; and God has graciously given you the lives of all that sail with you". So keep up your courage, men for I have faith in God that it will happen just as he told me" (Acts 27: 23-25).

Inspiring hope, faith and courage in others, Paul, the true

encourager, put his confidence in what God had said. Everyone on Paul's ship reached safety; not one was lost! They wintered in Malta for three months and then set sail for Rome. They probably did not get there any sooner than if they had spent the winter in Fair Havens, as God had directed. What a price they paid for disobedience!

Prayer

Lord, as I meditate upon Your Word, show me Your ways, teach me how to recognise Your voice and train me to obey promptly and fully. Amen.

A Question to Consider

Does God have some special advice or a directional word for you? Follow these steps:

1. **Wait on the Lord**
   - Decide when in your day you will sit quietly in solitude with the Lord. Stick to it. Switch off distractions.
   - Make that time and priority known to your family and request that they help you by giving you space and freedom from interruption.
   - Put up a "do not disturb" sign on your door and declare the same message to Satan! This is God's time.

2. **Pray and Meditate**
   - First, make sure your own heart is clean before the Lord. Ask the Holy Spirit to search your heart. Wait for Him to speak—do not rush this moment. Confess sin, repent and receive forgiveness.
   - Write down in your journal about what you are seeking God. It could be many things: a relationship, an opportunity, how to help your children, whether to go on a church outreach, etc.

a.   Write down what you already know about the
subject—facts, thoughts, etc.

- Ask the Holy Spirit to lead you to a passage of Scripture
to meditate on. Ponder the different thoughts and
passage(s) and ask the Holy Spirit to teach you.

    a.   During the following week, begin to study the
    passage thoroughly. Look up the meaning of
    different words.

    b.   To whom is the passage addressed? What is being
    said? When was it written? Why was it significant
    to the original audience? How does it apply to
    your life?

3.   The quickening of the Word

- Have confidence in God's ability to make His Word
known, rather than your ability to hear clearly.

- God will speak "just to you". Note what He is saying.

    a.   The Word is quickened within us; it will witness
    within.

- Continue to write down what you are learning.

    a.   Identify leading thoughts and list key points.

    b.   We reach a key moment when the Word begins to
    examine and study us.

    c.   Be ready to share in Life Group.

Life Group

- Have each group member read this Scripture as a prayer:
"Direct my steps by Your word, and let no iniquity have
dominion over me" (Psalm 119: 133 NKJV). Repeat the
process.

- About which matter are you seeking guidance? Share with the
group.

- To which Scripture(s) has God led you? Read it/ them to the group. What has God revealed through the Scripture(s)? Explain any insight and understanding which the Holy Spirit has given.
- Each one prays. Use the Scripture(s) received as a structure for prayer.

CHAPTER EIGHT

Overcoming Fear and Intimidation

"Walk in your God-given authority, or someone will
take it and use it against you." —John Bevere

From time to time, we have all battled against the spirit of fear and intimidation. For example, we may have felt afraid, attacked or felt small during an encounter, event or experience, without understanding why. Ignorant of the power and activity of evil spirits, it is likely we will attribute the fallout to our own weakness, or blame others, without discerning the evil source. This disruptive spirit tends to gain a foothold in the minds and hearts of believers who lack discernment because they have little knowledge of the truth of God's Word and how to apply it. Regular Biblical meditation will help rectify that!

Recognising Fear and Intimidation

The *spirit* of fear and intimidation is an evil spirit. Paul refers to it in 2 Timothy 1: 6-7. Satan assigns the spirit of fear to render believers spiritually ineffective. Operating in the spirit realm, it uses available human channels and all evil means to keep Christians self-centred and self-conscious, preventing them from discovering their identity, worth and potential in Christ Jesus.

It is common for the spirit of fear and intimidation to attack through authority figures in the world like politicians, law enforcers, bosses, teachers, parents, aunts and uncles. It can also operate through lawlessness—murderers, thugs, thieves and other aggressors. However, perhaps it is more unsettling to accept how this evil spirit operates through authority figures in our churches.

Using intimidation tactics, which belittle, ridicule and bully, this spirit plays on insecurities to threaten, manipulate and control relationships, destroying fellowship and restricting service. Those who have been subject to its brutal strength describe the experience as draining, isolating and confusing.

Examples of the Spirit of Fear at Work

- When we are afraid to speak up for fear of repercussions, the spirit of fear is at work.

- When we cannot recover from disappointments in life, or rise from failure in ministry or relationships, we are captive to the spirit of fear.

- When we cannot go to another to ask forgiveness for fear of negative reactions, we are submitting to the spirit of fear. It causes the fear of man.

- When we are afraid to speak out a word given by the Holy Spirit or use the gifts of the Holy Spirit, the spirit of fear has us in its grip.

- When we are afraid to say "no" for fear of rejection, we are submitting to the spirit of fear.

- The spirit of fear is intimidating us when we refuse to go to a particular location because of painful association.

The spirit of fear heightens awareness of our inadequacies. The words of discouraging voices ring in our ears and the consequences of past failures remain sharp in the memory. Fear keeps us from stepping out in faith, overstates the size of the task and causes us to doubt our capability to get it done. Intimidated by the spirit of fear we say, "No, sorry, I cannot do that, it is way beyond me".

A True Story: *That* Meeting

That specific meeting remains etched in the minds of Americans Val and Kristy.

Some years ago, whilst home from the mission field, a supporting church they had in common invited each to attend the annual business/prayer meeting. There were mission-related items on the agenda. During the meeting, there was heated debate about the mission budget. Val and Kristy listened closely; something was terribly wrong. The allocation of some mission support was misquoted. Mission funds had been "*re*allocated" to another local church project without the consent of the donor or church membership. Stirred to bring clarity without breaking confidence, Val stood to her feet. Members received what she said, but a deadly glare from the senior leader fired an intimidating warning across the room. Unwittingly, Val was uncovering a hidden personal agenda.

The following day, feeling very uneasy, she wrote a confidential letter to the church leaders explaining the concerns she had raised at the meeting. Kristy also chose to sign the letter.

Unwittingly, God had used them to expose a power struggle

within the leadership team and it instantly created a standoff. Behind the scenes, to divert attention from the wrongdoing, the senior leader instigated a campaign to intimidate, discredit and silence them.

A few weeks later, he invited them to a special meeting "with the wider leadership team to discuss the points raised in their letter". However, one hour before the meeting was due to start, the venue was unexpectedly changed and it emerged that only the senior leader would be present—the rest of the leadership team would be absent. The venue was now at the home of a local retired minister. He was a close friend of the senior leader but had nothing to do with the matter or the letter. Something underhand was at work.

Suspicious of motives and deeply concerned about their own well-being, Val and Kristy asked their senior mission leader to be present at the meeting. However, he was forbidden to attend. Only the retired minister and the senior leader would be present.

The authoritarian tone of the senior leader's opening statement made it clear that the above-mentioned business/prayer meeting, and the letter written by Val and Kristy, were not actually the reasons for convening the meeting. *Val and Kristy* were the agenda! For one hour, they endured belittling comments and unfounded accusations, which tore their hearts to shreds. They were dishonoured, demeaned and reprimanded like schoolchildren. Completely taken aback by the level of bullying, neither was able to speak in her defence. As the men stoically and dispassionately meted out the final blow, they remained unmoved by the distress they were causing. "You will no longer speak or participate in church publicly", they said.

Accordingly, in submission to the senior leader, they made no further contribution to the life of the church and remained quiet. The women had been intimidated and frightened into silence. Satan's job was done; the spirit of fear and intimidation had completed its destructive assignment. Val and Kristy were devastated but they chose to forgive. Meditating on Scriptures that affirmed them and brought healing, God faithfully restored them to ministry. Learning to trust leadership, however, took time.

This incident turned out to be one of many, which finally led to the demise of that congregation: more incidents of intimidation, manipulation and control were revealed, until the volcano finally erupted and the church splintered into many groups. When the spirit of fear and intimidation rules unchecked in any church, this is the outcome.

Overcoming the Spirit of Fear

> "Therefore I remind you to *stir up the gift of God* which is in you through the laying on of my hands. For God has not given us a spirit of fear, but of *power* and of *love* and of a *sound mind*" (2 Timothy 1: 6-7 NKJV, emphasis added).

God encourages us to be pro-active against the spirit of fear and intimidation wherever it manifests itself. We stand against lies and accusations by His power, responding in love and walking in truth.

1. Power Love and a Sound Mind

God has given us power, love and a sound mind, the opposite of what the spirit of fear brings—powerlessness, rejection and confusion.

a) Power

Paul reminds Timothy that he has received the power of God for ministry—"dunamis"—the miraculous strength, might and ability of God. Timothy had listened to the negative words of others concerning his age and ability and allowed the fire and passion of the Holy Spirit to be extinguished. Timothy needed reminding that he was living in disobedience by neglecting the power and anointing God had given.

We are to receive the Holy Spirit's power!

> "And He said to them, "It is not for you to know times or seasons which the Father has put in His own authority. But *you shall receive power* when the Holy Spirit has come upon you; and you shall be witnesses to Me in Jerusalem, and in all Judea and Samaria, and to the end of the earth."" (Acts 1: 7-8 NKJV, emphasis added).

Are we neglecting the miraculous power of God? Have the words of others snuffed out the fire in our heart, causing us to lay down a ministry to which we know God called us? Have we succumbed to the spirit of fear and the fear of man? God desires not only to show us His power, but also to show us His power operating *in and through* us.

> "But we have this treasure in earthen vessels, that the excellence of the power may be of God and not of us" (2 Corinthians 4: 7 NKJV).

b) Love

Love is the opposite of fear and is revealed in humility and the preferring of one another. Perfect love casts out fear. The choice, manner and tone of words will always give a clear indication of whether the Spirit of love or the spirit of fear is present. Are they words that build up and make us feel safe or do we feel belittled and afraid? Love always honours and secures, reassures and forgets wrongs; fear seeks to attack, tear down and control, and it has a long memory!

Learning to handle a dispute with someone who repeatedly intimidates us is crucial for spiritual growth. How should we handle their attacking, aggressive or argumentative manner? In the Kingdom of God relationship is always more valuable than being right, therefore, we should find ways to bless rather than to retaliate (Matthew 5: 39). We should humble ourselves and deliberately choose peace, refuse to argue and make the preservation of the relationship a priority.

> "There is no fear in love; but perfect love casts out fear, because fear involves torment. But he who fears has not been made perfect in love. We love Him because He first loved us" (1 John 4: 18-19 NKJV).

> "Love suffers long and is kind; love does not envy; love does not parade itself, is not puffed up; does not behave rudely, does not seek its own, is not provoked, thinks no evil; does not rejoice in iniquity, but rejoices in the truth; bears all things, believes all things, hopes all things, endures all things. Love never fails (1 Cor. 13: 4-8 NKJV).

c) Sound Mind

To have a sound mind means that we act with self-discipline—with soundness of mind. When the spirit of fear confuses and paralyses the mind it causes us to act impulsively and irrationally; we lose control and we say and do things which we later regret. We have the mind of Christ and therefore we have spiritual understanding, wisdom and ability to discern what is going on—what Satan and his spirits are up to (Proverbs 24: 3; Philippians 1: 9). By the Word and the Spirit, we can detect and refuse the lies of Satan with spiritual maturity and and self-control.

In that moment of attack we need to step back, look to the Lord and consciously make a choice. We can focus on the lies and accusations directed towards us, or we can choose to come in the opposite spirit, a Christ-like spirit, with truth *and love*.

> "Now we have received, not the spirit of the world, but the Spirit who is from God, that we might know the things that have been freely given to us by God. These things we also speak, not in words which man's wisdom teaches but which the Holy Spirit teaches, comparing spiritual things with spiritual. But the natural man does not receive the things of the Spirit of God, for they are foolishness to him; nor can he know them, because they are spiritually discerned. But he who is spiritual judges all things, yet he himself is rightly judged by no one. For "who has known the mind of the LORD that he may instruct Him?" *But we have the mind of Christ*" (1 Corinthians 2: 12-16 NKJV emphasis added).

In this context, meditation on other Scriptures that speak of God's power, love and self-control will build up a strong deposit of truth which can be declared with authority to defeat Satan.

2. Take your Rightful Place

We must never surrender our position of authority in Christ to the spirit of fear and intimidation. Do not treat Satan with respect and behave as if we are under his power. Satan will use fear tactics to magnify his presence and make us believe that we are subservient to him. We are not subject or subservient to him or evil spirits.

God has raised Jesus up from the dead and seated Him at His right hand in the heavenly places, *far above* principalities, powers, might and dominion (Ephesians 1: 20-21). Therefore, because we are *in Christ Jesus* we also have received authority, position and power over principalities and powers. This includes the spirit of fear and intimidation.

We must enforce our authority and position over the spirit of fear in each situation. As this spirit operates through people, even Christians, we must choose to fear God and not man. By wrongfully fearing man, we surrender our positon and authority in Christ. Meditation on Scriptures, like Ephesians 1: 20-21, which teach of our inheritance in Christ, will help strengthen belief and develop spiritual resolve to stand ground against Satan's intimidating tactics.

3. Stir up the Gift of God

God gives spiritual gifts to individuals to build up the Body of Christ. Often, because of fear, they lie dormant. We do not step out in faith because we fear being "wrong" or "judged". Therefore, by stirring up the gift of God and using it, we release the power of the Spirit for the blessing and growth of others and conquer the spirit of fear. Faith and obedience to God always breaks the power of fear.

> "Therefore I remind you to *stir up the gift of God* which is in you through the laying on of my hands. For God has not given us a spirit of fear, but of power and of love and of a sound mind" (2 Timothy 1: 6-7 NKJV, emphasis added).

To "stir up" means to kindle afresh or keep in full flame. A flame with no oxygen dies; spiritual oxygen is the Holy Spirit. Paul was saying to Timothy, "Your gift and calling are dormant because timidity has gripped your heart; stir up the gift of God!"

4. Repent and Forgive

Unforgiveness and the consequent bitterness, gives the spirit of fear and intimidation a foothold from which Satan can wreak havoc in our lives. When hurt and in the taking of offence, it is likely that we will sin in our responses. Forgiving quickly prevents a root of bitterness from developing; lingering resentment leads to bitterness.

Therefore, we need to:

- Repent of yielding to the spirit of fear and thus disobeying God.
- Forgive those who have hurt or offended us.

5. Praise and Worship God

Fear focuses on man; praise focuses on God. Therefore, another powerful weapon for overcoming the spirit of fear and intimidation is praise. Declaring the Word of God in praise is powerful. We are to have the "high praises of God in our mouths *and a two-edged sword in our hand*" (Psalm 149: 5-6, emphasis added). This is not a onetime praise session; it is *a lifestyle* of praise and thankfulness, which keeps the enemy in his place.

- Praise opens the door for God to invade every situation; He confuses the plans of the enemy and defeats him (2 Chronicles 20: 22).
- Praise is something we must choose to do; if we listen to our flesh we will only complain.

Heartfelt praise declares the reign of God (Psalm 22: 3-4). He "inhabits" the praises of His people. "Inhabits," means He sits down, remains and settles. His presence abides with us in a growing relationship. Many times choosing to praise is a sacrifice in obedience to God. Continuous praise of God fixes our hearts and minds on His greatness and stirs up faith in Him. Inviting God into our circumstances in this manner powerfully breaks shackles of darkness, which seek to dominate our souls (mind, will and emotions).

David declared, "I will praise You!"

"I will praise You, O LORD, with my whole heart; I will tell of all Your marvellous works. I will be glad and rejoice in You; I will sing praise to Your name, O Most High" (Psalm 9: 1-2 NKJV).

"You shall fear the LORD your God; you shall serve Him, and to Him you shall hold fast, and take oaths in His name. He is your praise, and He is your God, who has done for you these great and awesome things which your eyes have seen" (Deuteronomy 10: 20-21 NKJV).

Moses

Moses was familiar with intimidation and fear. Though a Hebrew, he was raised as a son of Pharaoh in Egypt. He killed an Egyptian, thinking that no-one had seen him. When he realised his secret was known, he fled in fear (Exodus 2: 14-15) and settled in Midian as a shepherd. There, God appeared to Moses in a burning bush (Exodus 3: 1-2), appointing him to deliver Israel from the bondage and slavery of Egypt (Exodus 3: 9-10).

As soon as God spoke, Moses responded with his excuses: I'm a nobody; they won't believe me (Exodus 4: 1); I am not eloquent; I am slow of speech (Exodus 4: 10); my track record isn't great—please send someone else (Exodus 4: 13). Moses was intimidated by his own weaknesses, inabilities, past failure and Pharaoh's wrath. The spirit of fear and intimidation threatened to keep Moses from his God-given destiny to lead Israel out of slavery and bondage. God taught him that spiritual success lies in meditating upon His character, nature and abilities.

Jezebel, Ahab and Elijah

Jezebel had such a controlling and intimidating spirit that King Ahab (her husband), the leaders and all the people of Israel gave way to her. Even Elijah, the great prophet, yielded to the spirit operating through her and fled. On Mt. Carmel he stood against the mighty prophets of Baal and prevailed (1 Kings 18: 19–19: 3), yet ran away at the name of Jezebel! He feared the woman and ended up sacrificing the fear of the Lord, inner peace, courage, confidence and even the joy of victory.

Summary

The spirit of fear and intimidation is a very strong and deceptive spirit. When attacked, strength and courage dissipate and it is hard to pray or read the Word. However, that is exactly the time when we need to be more aware of the Lord's presence, not less. Moving against the tide of feelings, we must stir our soul to increase engagement with God in praise, worship, prayer and Biblical meditation. We must also walk in the fear of the Lord, and walk in love. An ever-increasing experience of love *from* God, and love *for* God, leaves no room for fear to find a place in our minds and hearts. Perfect love drives out fear—fear of man, fear of failure, fear of making a scene, fear of retribution, fear of inadequacies—whatever.

"Perfect love casts out fear" (1 John 4: 17-18 NKJV).

"Be zealous for the fear of the Lord all day long" (Proverbs 23: 17 NKJV).

Preparation for Life Group

- Spend time meditating on the following passage: 1 Samuel 17: 1-57
- Print the passage on an A4 sheet. This will be used in Life Group.

Life Group Meditation: David and Goliath

This Biblical meditation will confirm:

1. The nature of intimidation
2. How it operates
3. Through whom it operates
4. What disarms its power

Without opening your Bibles, recount the story of 1 Samuel 17: 1-57. Allow a free flow of comment and contribution. Group facilitator: Hand out the A4 copy of the Scripture passage.

- Read the passage together slowly.

    a. Underline the main players in this scene.
    b. Place a box around words or phrases which are intimidating. For example 1 Samuel 17: 4 "A champion went out …. Whose height was six cubits and a span" By the way, that is 9 feet 9 inches!

- What was so intimidating about Goliath?

- Describe in your own words the effect of intimidation. How did the people in the story react?

- What do you conclude about Eliab's attitude?

  a. Reflect on what happened to Eliab when Samuel went to Bethlehem to anoint the next king of Israel (1 Samuel 16: 1-7).
  b. Read 1 Samuel 17: 28.

- What do you know about David from both 1 Samuel 16: 11-13 and the passage you have read?

  a. Summarise his characteristics. For example: Youngest, smallest …
  b. How did David's response to Goliath differ from that of others? Why?

- What is the importance of David using the term "uncircumcised Philistine"? (1 Samuel 17: 26; 36)

- How did King Saul describe David? (1 Samuel 17: 31-37)

- What did King Saul offer David by way of protection?
  a. Discuss the difference between what was offered and what David used (1 Samuel 17: 38-40).
  b. Discuss how Goliath viewed his opponent (1 Samuel 17: 42-44). How did he try to intimidate David?
  c. What spiritual armour did David eventually use? (1 Samuel 17: 45-47) Discuss why he made that choice.

- What does this story teach us about confronting the spirit of fear?

Application

1. Describe situations, or characteristics in people, which intimidate and fill you with fear. Why are you intimdated?
2. Has fear and intimidation held you back from being obedient to the Lord?

- Describe what happened. What caused your heart's resolve to fail? Why did you fear? Why did you flee? How did you feel afterwards?
- Now that you have studied this chapter, what does God want you to do?
- Pray together.

A Prayer of Repentance and Healing

Use this prayer, which we have adapted from "Fashioned for Glory" by Yanit Ross, to end group time. First, read it through together, and then invite each one to pray relevant portions to express their heart to God.

"Father, please expose and remove any insecurities in my life which have given the spirit of intimidation a place to attack me. Please heal any wounds, which would cause me to yield to people pleasing and to a need for the approval of man. Meet my needs for love, acceptance and approval. Please purify my heart; cleanse me from all sin."

"I repent of allowing others to have control over me, and of yielding to a spirit of intimidation. I repent of disobeying You. I repent of despising and neglecting the spiritual gifts and leadership You entrusted to me. Today I confess and renounce fear. I rebuke the spirit of fear and intimidation and command it to leave me in Jesus' name!"

"I nullify all words of control and intimidation spoken over my life by myself and others. I break the spirit of the fear of man from me in Jesus' name. I submit to God and I resist the spirit of fear. Go in Jesus' name. You have no place in my life."

"I command every national spirit of control and intimidation to leave me in Jesus' name! I belong to the kingdom of God and will be ruled by the Lord Jesus Christ and not by the spirit over _____ (name the nation). I am not under your rule; I am under the reign of King Jesus! Lord Jesus, please sit on the throne of my heart and rule me from within. I declare You as my Lord."

"Father, please help me to stir up the gifts You have given me. Give me greater understanding of my authority in You, and teach me to walk in Your power, Your love and Your soundness of thinking."

"Thank You! In the name of Jesus, the Messiah, amen."

(Yanit Ross: Fashioned For Glory- Restored and Equipped through Biblical Counselling and Prayer)

CHAPTER NINE

Enduring Suffering

"Suffering is not an accident, but a gift to be cherished. For, when properly received it works to enhance ones eternal rank, fame and honour." —Paul Bilheimer

In this book, we have taken you on a journey to discover the creative and life-changing power of Biblical meditation. Now I, Mintie, want to share my personal story with you. For me, Biblical meditation is much more than a spiritual discipline, which I know I am commanded to live out; it is the very heartbeat of life itself. I have discovered that the reward of a reflective, diligent and purposeful meditation on His Word is beautiful intimacy with my heavenly Father. I haven't always thought this way, but the path of suffering has led me to the fullness of this truth.

In 1973, I was called by God to leave South Africa and go to Israel. Once I had heard the Lord, I was resolute and planned my way in obedience. Nothing could hold me back; I was a plump, strong, confident and energetic 23 year old on a mission with God. I couldn't speak Hebrew, so upon arrival in Israel, I enrolled in a language school—"Ulpan"—in Natanya, on the Mediterranean Sea and loved it! I was the only Gentile among 35 Jews who had recently immigrated (made "Aliyah"). This was my first contact with Jewish people who were returning to Israel, the Land of Promise, and this Scripture came alive.

"And He who formed you, O Israel: "Fear not, for I have redeemed you; I have called you by your name; You are Mine. When you pass through the waters, I will be with you; and through the rivers, they shall not overflow you. When you walk through the fire, you shall not be burned, nor shall the flame scorch you. For I am the LORD your God, the Holy One of Israel, your Saviour; I gave Egypt for your ransom, Ethiopia and Seba in your place. Since you were precious in My sight, you have been honoured, and I have loved you; therefore I will give men for you, and people for your life. *Fear not, for I am with you; I will bring your descendants from the east, and gather you from the west; I will say to the north, 'Give them up!' And to the south, 'Do not keep them back!' Bring My sons from afar, and My daughters from the ends of the earth*—everyone who is called by My name, whom I have created for My glory; I have formed him, yes, I have made him""" (Isaiah 43: 1-7, NKJV, emphasis added).

The first five weeks of language study flew by and our hard work rewarded with a weekend off. I chose to spend time with Christian friends in the Galilee. On the Friday, during the last lesson, I suddenly became aware of a gritty feeling in my eyes. It was as if sand were falling into them, making it nearly impossible to see. Noticing my dilemma, one of the students helped me to the bus station to make the journey to the Galilee. My eyes became increasingly swollen and red. That night fever gripped my body. By morning I was paralysed; I could not walk, and had intense pain, fever and swelling in my joints.

That Saturday afternoon I experienced several small heart attacks and by evening, my condition was acute. My South African friends, Piet and Rita Kotze, telephoned the doctor from Kibbutz Ashdod Yaakov in the Jordan Valley, where Piet was employed.

Immediately, Penicillin to which I had an immediate and severe allergic reaction was prescribed. My skin was inflamed with welts.

By Monday, the fever, paralysis and pain were unrelenting; I was critically ill. In the corner of the bedroom I saw a dark and forbidding demonic being intent on taking my life (John 10: 10), however, I strongly resisted giving in to the intense attack. Tannie Anna Venter (Auntie Anna), with whom I was staying, advised that my mother and father in South Africa be informed, but I pleaded with her not to call them because I knew I was going to come through.

On Wednesday, a prayer alert was raised. Piet Kotze, who had been seeking the Lord about what to do, came into the room and commanded me to "get up and walk in Jesus' name". I could not walk, but the authority in his voice told me I had better try! Gingerly, fighting the pain and extreme weakness, I shuffled across the room and back to my bed. We all hoped that this was the beginning of change, but by the end of the week, I was urgently transferred to the Mission Hospital in Nazareth. The doctor informed me that I had both scarlet and rheumatic fever, and advised that I return to South Africa as soon as possible to be treated and cared for.

The Lord had sent me to Israel and only He could instruct me by His Word. The thought of heading home on the word of a doctor seemed utterly wrong. I argued my point and refused to comply. However, later that week, as I was praying, I heard the tender voice of the Lord say, "Mintie, go down to the south". I persisted with my argument, "But Lord, I need a word from Your Word before I will move. Surely You are not sending me back?" Within a matter of moments Acts 8: 26-27 came to mind: ""*Arise and go toward the south* along the road which goes down from Jerusalem to Gaza." This is desert. So he arose and went."

I know it says "Gaza", but I knew God meant South Africa! Reluctantly, I flew home and the South African doctors at Tygerberg

Hospital, Cape Town, provided medical care. Further blood tests revealed I had severe rheumatoid arthritis. The prognosis was grim. RA is a chronic auto-immune disease that causes chronic inflammation of the joints and severe disability. There was no cure but the inflammation and pain could be controlled with medication. All of it was hard to accept.

My health had deteriorated quickly; dark clouds gathered over my heart and mind. The illness was one thing, but the disappointment of returning to South Africa so soon after being sent out by the Lord was too much to bear. I had so many unanswered questions about my future. Actually, I feared I would never return to Israel. I couldn't walk, lift or bathe myself; I was confined to a wheelchair. When eventually my hair fell out, I felt utterly stripped of life, dignity and purpose. I was trapped, thwarted in the prime of life. It never occurred to me to blame God, but I was certainly very angry with Satan.

Christians bombarded me with accusations that it was my sin that had caused the affliction. I repented of anything and everything I could think of, but there was no miracle of physical healing. Healing was not going to happen that way for me; God had a very different plan. I took every opportunity to attend healing meetings for the laying on of hands, but the RA continued to deform the joints, particularly in my hands, neck and feet. As the Lord whispered into my spirit, "Mintie, I am going to purify you through suffering—you will know the joy of my strength being cultivated in you", a growing peace settled me down. The Lord could be trusted!

Doubts surfaced, but God once again spoke to me through His Word, "Mintie, My grace is sufficient for you and My strength will be made perfect in weakness" (2 Corinthians 12: 9). They were not the words I wanted to hear. However, I had a strong feeling that God wanted to teach me lessons, which my strong will and tough constitution would not learn in any other way. Desperation for God to help led me to discover a new dimension of intimacy with God through Biblical meditation. The Word became my medicine.

The Lord was sharing revelations about Himself, which I could only learn as I wrestled with Him through my suffering. Those were lessons designed not just for my good but for those whom I would eventually disciple. I was young in the Lord and knew so little about endurance, because I had never had to endure; I knew so little about overcoming, because I had not experienced many hurdles; I knew so little about God's faithfulness, because I would never really had needs I could not meet. Now, struck down by a chronic illness, which threatened to overwhelm and sink my life, I had some decisions to make. Do I submit to the rheumatoid arthritis and let this disease define me and dictate my future, or do I let God teach me His higher way of faith, trust and spiritual adventure? I chose the latter.

> "This is a faithful saying: For if we died with Him, We shall also live with Him. If we endure, we shall also reign with Him. If we deny Him, He also will deny us. If we are faithless, He remains faithful; He cannot deny Himself" (2 Timothy 2: 11-13 NKJV).

When I left Tygerberg Hospital, I stayed with my parents. With growing confidence in the Lord's strength, I started to take small steps in my bedroom, hanging on to furniture for dear life. I often fell, but helped by family members I always got up to try again. Eventually, I could walk unaided, albeit slowly and stiffly. My heart was set on returning to Israel. If my health would only allow me to go for short periods, that is how it would be, but I fervently believed that one day I would return to the Promised Land to stay.

Between 1974 and 1983, by God's grace and strength, I visited Israel, staying for periods of 7 to 9 months before returning to South Africa for more treatment. Eventually in 1983, despite all the challenges of rheumatoid arthritis, I finally returned to Israel with the blessing of my pastor, Ed Roebert, of Hatfield Baptist Church, Pretoria, South Africa. God had allowed me to be part of a team that was to establish Peniel Fellowship, a new Messianic fellowship in the Galilee. I helped disciple women. Later, from 1985 – 1991, I worked as the bursar of the Garden Tomb, Jerusalem. The Garden Tomb is believed by many to be the garden and sepulchre of Joseph of Arimathea, and therefore possibly the burial and resurrection site of Jesus.

I continuously struggled with pain, which made me very tired, but I had within me an enabling power that was greater than my weariness! I soared in the Spirit; my spirit was buoyed. How true the Aaronic blessing is: "The Lord lifted His countenance upon me and gave me peace" (Numbers 6: 22-26). How glad I was that His face shone upon me, not my pain. Serving the Lord in Israel among His chosen people made my joy complete.

Nobody was more surprised than I was, when, in 1990 the Lord started to prepare my heart to leave Israel. God awakens our ear to hear when we regularly meditate on God's Word. God is able to prime and speak through passages, stories and the lives of the patriarchs and apostles. For some time I had meditated productively on the following Scriptures:

"For out of Zion the law shall go forth, and the word of the LORD from Jerusalem" (Micah 4: 2 NKJV).

"And Jesus came and spoke to them, saying, "All authority has been given to Me in heaven and on earth. Go therefore and *make disciples of all the nations*, baptising them in the name of the Father and of the Son and of the Holy Spirit, teaching them to observe all things that I have commanded you; and lo, I am with you always, even to the end of the age." Amen" (Matthew 28: 18-20, NKJV, emphasis added).

It was time. He was sending me to disciple the nations, and to share about God's chosen people, Israel. I didn't have any more details, but I knew from experience that I didn't need many because God was with me. He knew what was ahead, He knew my special needs and He knew my limitations. In 1990, I travelled to Lausanne, Switzerland, to participate in a three-month Crossroads Discipleship Training School with Youth with a Mission. As the School split into small "flock-groups" I was placed under the leadership of Jan Whitmore (née Rowland). We soon became friends, but neither realised this was no chance encounter, it was God's appointment. After the School, I went back to Israel, and Jan continued training with YWAM.

In March 1991, whilst sitting in my apartment in Jerusalem, I contemplated God's directive to "go to the nations". My spirit was stirred. I prayed, "Lord, I am willing to go, but You know my weak frame, I cannot go alone. Who will go with me, who will help me?" No sooner had I uttered the words than the telephone rang. It was Jan calling from England.

> "Mintie, I had to call you. This morning as I was praying and waiting on the Lord, I sensed God ask me the question: "Jan, will you look after Mintie for Me?" I have no idea what this means, but does it mean anything to you?"

Tears trickled down my cheeks. Once again, God, who knew my weak frame, was providing help for the journey. I knew that before I could "go to the nations" my hands needed surgery, and, I knew I would need someone to help me. Later that year, Jan accompanied me to South Africa for an operation to reconstruct my deformed hands. As both hands were incapacitated and I could do nothing for myself, Jan took care of all my personal needs. After having completed her nursing duties, she returned to Youth with a Mission (YWAM) in the USA and I returned to Israel.

The following year, in April 1992, God purposed that we meet again, when we independently applied for the same YWAM Pastoral Support School in Nuneaton, UK. Following training, we became co-workers in the encouragement of YWAM missionaries in Eastern Europe. We were based.at the YWAM base in Lausanne, Switzerland, where we had first met in 1990.

In pursuit of our mission of encouragement, I was able to bring revelation about God's divine purposes for Israel, and the Holy Spirit led us to missionaries working for organisations associated with the prophesied return of the Jews to Israel. Isn't God amazing? He had orchestrated the whole thing!

Looking back, I have to acknowledge God's amazing ways. In the natural, very few Christian missions would ever have accepted me for mission work because of my disability. However, God was not concerned about that. God, through Jan and others, enables me to run the race that He has set before me.

We may think that God's agenda is about *doing* something on His behalf, but I have learned through suffering that God's higher agenda is intimacy with Him and transformation not achievement. God uses suffering to break pride and transform us into His image. I often reflect on the shepherd who lovingly breaks the leg of a wilful sheep that it would learn to be dependent and secure.

Suffering comes in many forms but it isn't to be feared. The restriction and confinement that it may bring, does not necessarily mean that God is judging us. The suffering, if embraced, ultimately empowers and frees us to know God intimately. Sure, I am physically hampered, but through Biblical meditation I have learned from God that my illness does not need to dictate or define my worth, purpose or quality of life. Although many speak of the peaceful radiance of the Lord, they see in me, I can only give glory to God for His strength, which enables me gracefully to endure and overcome physical limitations. The Holy Spirit has taught me how to draw strength and consolation from God's wonderful Word.

> "But what things were gain to me, these I have counted loss for Christ. Yet indeed *I also count all things loss for the excellence of the knowledge of Christ Jesus my Lord, for whom I have suffered the loss of all things,* and count them as rubbish, that I may gain Christ and be found in Him, not having my own righteousness, which is from the law, but that which is through faith in Christ, the righteousness which is from God by faith; that I may know Him and the power of His resurrection, and the fellowship of His sufferings, being conformed to His death, if, by any means, I may attain to the resurrection from the dead" (Philippians 3: 7-11 NKJV, emphasis added).

What a contrast between the physical life and life in the Spirit. They are vastly different. In my flesh, there is frustration and limitation, but in the Spirit, there is unlimited liberty and joy, which can endure any storm. God is so utterly confident of His ability and power working in and through me that He still assigns special tasks to me, even in weakness. At 65, having had a chronic illness for 41 years, I still regularly deposit the Word in my heart through Biblical meditation and live by the strength of that indwelling Word. I still "go" because God says He will enable me! As the Word is the voice of God, I hear my Saviour encourage me all the way. It is a daily supernatural miracle. Where would I have been had the Word not been deposited in me? I would have run round in circles on empty! Many times, I meditated on this verse:

"Do not sorrow, for the joy of the LORD is your strength" (Nehemiah 8: 10b NKJV)

Many who see my crooked frame say, "How do you carry on, Mintie?" The answer is probably more practical than one might imagine. When I cannot walk, and there are many such days, I sit down and meditate upon God; we meet face to face. When I cannot get up in the morning because of stiffness, I lie back into His arms and pray for others. When frustration and pain are overwhelming and everything drops through my crooked hands, I lift them up to the Lord, call upon His name and shout to Jan for help. When I feel useless because I don't have the physical capacity of others, I rejoice and thank the Lord for what I can do, and let go of the things I cannot do. I take God at His word. When He says, "Fix your eyes on Me", I do so; when He says, "Lay aside every weight that holds you back", I offload; when He says, "Come unto Me all you who are weary and heavy laden", I flop back into His loving arms.

I no longer pray to be free of suffering; I pray to know the Lord more intimately in the midst of it. Suffering has blessed me with untold discoveries of God, His immense love, amazing provision and His divine protection. I wonder how many can say they are *that* rich or even *that* healed?

"The LORD is my strength and my shield; my heart trusted in Him, and I am helped; therefore my heart greatly rejoices, and with my song I will praise Him. The LORD is their strength, and He is the saving refuge of His anointed. Save Your people, and bless Your inheritance; shepherd them also, and bear them up forever" (Psalm 28: 7-9 NKJV).

A Meditation Prayer

"Lord, give ear to my words and consider my meditation. Give heed to the voice of my cry, my King and my God, for to You I will pray. My voice You shall hear in the morning, O LORD; in the morning I will direct it to You, and I will look up. Let the words of my mouth and the meditation of my heart be acceptable in Your sight, O LORD, my strength and my Redeemer.

O, how I love Your law! I will make it my meditation all the day. You, through Your commandments, make me wiser than my enemies, for they are ever with me. Thank You that I have more understanding than all my teachers because Your testimonies are my meditation. I meditate on all Your work and I will talk of Your deeds. I will also meditate on Your precepts, and contemplate Your ways. I will not forget Your Word. Even in the night watches, I will meditate on the glorious splendour of Your majesty, and on Your name.

Lord, I never want Your glorious Book to depart from my mouth. Constantly remind me to meditate in it day and night, and observe to do according to all that is written in it". Amen.

(Extracts used from: Psalm 5: 1-3; Psalm 19: 14; Psalm 119: 97-99; Psalm 77: 12; Psalm 119: 15-16; Psalm 119: 148; Psalm 145: 5; Malachi 3: 16; Joshua 1: 8 NKJV)

Preparation for Life Group

- How have you suffered?

- What Scriptures or aspects of truth have helped you endure suffering?

Life Group

- Share your story of suffering and the Scriptures which guided and sustained you.

  o What did God teach you?

- This is the last week of the study on Biblical meditation.

  o Take time to pray for each one.
  o Make a fresh commitment to digest, uphold and honour God's Word.
  o Give thanks and praise to God for the fellowship enjoyed.
  o Plan to have a "bring and share" meal within a few weeks.

Mintie Nel & Jan Whitmore

APPENDIX ONE

Forming A Life Group

As this is the first time you are with others who will share your 9-week journey of spiritual growth, it is good to begin by reading Appendix 1 together as a group. Take a few minutes to introduce yourselves, and then ask one person to read aloud for all to enjoy.

We are passionate about small, committed discipleship groups which meet together *in a structured and purposeful way* to facilitate an exciting environment for spiritual growth. Every opportunity you take to share what God has been teaching you will accelerate your own spiritual development. The members of the life group should commit to systematically follow the study and meet on a regular basis. Group members can decide the frequency of meetings. Some groups may want to meet weekly for a 9-week discipleship season; others may prefer to meet every two weeks, extending the discipleship season to 18 weeks. You can be flexible in the use of the material, as long as *all* members of the life group agree.

It would be beneficial for the life group to do the following today:

- decide who leads the group;
- decide what the purpose of the group is;
- decide on frequency of meetings;
- decide where to meet;
- decide how best to study;
- hear members express their expectations for the group; and
- hear how members would like to use the materials.

Agree from the outset that the life group is not about eating and drinking. Enjoy tea, coffee, or a cold drink and a plate of biscuits, but keep it simple. The focus of the life group is fellowship around the discipleship study, not food. At the end of the season of growing together, you may want to share a special meal during which you reflect on the time spent together and how it affected your life.

Group size: Don't make the group any larger than *four or five people*. A larger group inhibits sharing at a deeper level. If the group is larger, meet in two or three separate groups within the same location. At the end of the session, the groups can come back together to share the joy of what has been experienced.

Commitment: Each member should commit to making the life group a priority for the duration of the course. Partial attendance does not work well. A bond of love, honour, respect, and understanding is established when *all* fulfil what has been agreed upon. The opposite is also true: group spirit languishes when some participate half-heartedly or display indifference to the life group time. When members have more important commitments at exactly the time of your life group, it devalues the commitment made and dishonours fellow group members. So whatever agreement you make, all should stick to it! Obviously there are genuine reasons for non-attendance, such as sickness or an emergency, but agree to let the group know. Where possible, the meeting time can be changed. Our purpose is to cut out the lame excuses! Satan specialises in such, which introduce apathy and indifference. These times of meeting and sharing will become precious, and build meaningful relationships which last.

Plan ahead: Diarise your meetings, each no longer than two hours. This gives fifteen minutes for everyone to arrive and settle and fifteen minutes at the end to enjoy some simple refreshments. One and a half hours should be guarded for sharing aspects of the discipleship study and for prayer.

Agree to switch off phones: Try to meet where the telephone can be silenced and have group members switch off their mobile phones. Don't just put them on silent with vibration; switch them off. This is hallowed time together. In this way, you honour the Lord and the people with whom you are. Normally there is nothing which cannot wait two hours!

Group confidentiality: Many of the life group questions are penetrating and personal. It is crucial that the group understands and abides by *confidentiality*. Nothing that was shared should be mentioned outside the group unless you have the person's permission.

Be real: When sharing, try not to use spiritual clichés, use everyday language. Allow group members to share without interruption. Learn to listen to others and not be wholly consumed with what you want to say. As you listen to others, pray for them. It is not easy to make yourself vulnerable at this level, but the rewards of a closer and richer fellowship are immense.

Question and feedback: After uninterrupted sharing has finished, take some time to exchange questions and give feedback. Debate was a normal and healthy part of the life of disciples in Jesus' day and an essential way to learn. However, we must learn when debating to disagree respectfully and without tantrum or taking offence. Remember, we are co-disciples – we are all learners.

Freedom: Many meetings will conclude with confession in prayer. Allow time for each one to pray. When the Holy Spirit starts to touch hearts, revealing weaknesses and failures, it can become emotional. People feel vulnerable and exposed, and there may be weeping. Please allow your fellow group members to weep and mourn their sin without any intervention. At this stage, don't halt their repentance. Be empathetic, supportive and merciful, and give space.

Stay focused: When praying for each other, keep prayers centred on what was shared. Don't drift into other topics. Be honest with one another when this happens. Use this opportunity to pick up on some of the desires which each have shared and express them to the Lord. Make sure everyone in the group receives prayer. If you run out of time, start with those who haven't been prayed for next time you meet.

APPENDIX TWO

A Guide to Meditating

Upon The Word Of God

The following steps will help prepare the way for meeting with God and allowing Him to engraft His Word into your heart. These are simple steps, which may be practiced alone or in a small group. To help facilitate the exercise you may wish to print the passage of Scripture on a piece of A4 paper.

Preparation for Meditation

Place:
- Find and designate the space where you will be alone with God. You have a divine appointment.

Switch off:
- Switch off your mobile telephone. You are not available.

Settle down:
- Find a comfortable position, close your eyes and breathe deeply.

Turn towards God:
- Lift your face and incline your heart towards God. Let your physical body lean back, raise your hands and hold that position for two minutes.
- Pray and give thanks: "Thank you, Lord Jesus, for being here". Repeat this phrase several times. You are becoming conscious of God's presence. Linger a while.

Thankfulness:
- Open your Bible to the chosen passage for meditation.
- Lay your hand on the text and thank the Lord for His precious Word. As you do so, consciously commit to concentrating only upon the Word of God. Don't allow

yourself to drift away into other imagery. This meditation is upon God and His Word.

- Thank Him that His divine Word has power over every work of the enemy. Thank Him that He desires to speak to you. Thank Him for the insight He will bring.

Ask:

- Ask the Holy Spirit to lead you in this meditation and sit quietly before the Lord.

The Process of Meditation

Read:

- Read through the complete Scripture passage three times
- On the fourth time, read it aloud. You are intentionally centring your meditation on the chosen verses.

Wait:

- Sit quietly before the Lord and ask the Holy Spirit to speak to you through the verses.
- Drink in His presence as you read the passage.
- Write in your notebook the first thoughts which stir in your mind.
- Underline words which stand out.

Consider who, what, why, when, how:

- Read the passage aloud at least four more times. Read slowly, considering each word. Ask the Holy Spirit to teach you what each word or phrase is saying.
- Now read it again, pausing at the end of each sentence or phrase. Allow different words or ideas to touch your spirit.
- Who was there? What was happening? What is the overall message? Which adjectives (descriptive words) are used?

Why are certain phrases used? How does the writer relate to God?

The Character of God:

- What does the passage reveal about the character of God?

Applying Meditation

New title:

- Give the passage of Scripture your own title. What would you call it and why?

Rewrite:

- Re-write the passage in your own words. What is God saying to you personally?

Compose a prayer:

- Write a prayer which reflects the heart of the meaning of the passage.

Pray the Scripture:

- Declare/speak out your prayer to the Lord.

Sing the Scripture:

- Put words and phrases from the Scripture passage to a melody. Sing a new song! Even if it is a song on one note, let your spirit sing the Word!

Give thanks:

- Give thanks for the time you have enjoyed with the Lord. Express your desire that the divine truth of these verses be engrafted into your heart.

Develop and share your meditation:

- During the coming days, regularly return to the verses of meditation. Ask the Holy Spirit to enlarge your understanding and give more insight.
- Share insights with a trusted friend.

Act on your meditation:

- Is there something you need to repent of?
- What changes do you need to make to your life?
- Is there an act of obedience you must fulfil?
- Is there an act of service you must do for someone else?

Face to Face with God

APPENDIX THREE

Seven Bible Meditations

To Strengthen Faith

Meditation One

Safety of Abiding in the Presence of God

"He who dwells in the secret place of the Most High shall abide under the shadow of the Almighty. I will say of the LORD, "He is my refuge and my fortress; my God, in Him I will trust"" (Psalm 91: 1-2 NKJV).

- God is described as Most High—"Elyon", and Almighty—"Shaddai", meaning He is all-sufficient, all-powerful, mighty and unconquerable.
- The descriptions signify God's greatness, strength and everlasting nature. He has the capacity and the capability of being all that His people need.
- Where does this Scripture say we dwell? What does this mean in our everyday lives?
- Read verses 3-13. What does God deliver us from when we shelter in Him?
- Read verses 9-16. What are the blessings of choosing the Lord as our refuge?

Pray the Scripture

Lord, I place my life in Your hands. Thank you that I am under Your protective care. You are my refuge and fortress; my God, in You I will trust. Amen.

Meditation Two

You are the God Who Sees—El-Roi

"Then she called the name of the LORD who spoke to her, You-Are-the-God-Who-Sees; for she said, "Have I also here seen Him who sees me?" 14 Therefore the well was called Beer Lahai Roi; observe, it is between Kadesh and Bered" (Genesis 16: 13-14 NKJV).

The promised heir to Abram and Sarai had not materialised, so they devised their own scheme, which the New Testament describes as "according to the flesh" (Galatians 4: 23). Sarai gave Abram her maid Hagar, and she bore him a son, Ishmael.

- Read Genesis 16: 1-46. Who are the main characters in the story?
- What did God "see"?
- Have you "seen Him who sees us"?
- How would seeing God influence your life?

Pray the Scripture

Thank you that You see exactly where I am located and what is happening in my life. Open my spiritual eyes to see You and meet You face to face. Amen.

Meditation Three

I Am Who I Am—Yahweh, LORD

"And God said to Moses, "I AM WHO I AM." And He said, "Thus you shall say to the children of Israel, 'I AM has sent me to you.'" 15 Moreover God said to Moses, "Thus you shall say to the children of Israel: 'The LORD God of your fathers, the God of Abraham, the God of Isaac, and the God of Jacob, has sent me to you. This is My name forever, and this is My memorial to all generations.'" (Exodus 3: 14-15 NKJV).

- Read the entire story, Exodus 3: 1-22.
  - ○ Where was Moses (v1)?
  - ○ How did God describe the place and how did He announce Himself (v5-6)?
- "So I have come down" (v8) and "Now therefore, I will send you" (v10)
  - ○ What does this reveal about the way in which God works out His plans?
- When Moses says, "Who am I?" (v11), how does God answer him?

When God asks us to act on His behalf, He sees, hears, knows, goes with us and instructs us step by step.

Pray the Scripture

Lord, I choose not to use my weaknesses as excuses, but say, "I am Yours, use me as You will". Amen.

Meditation Four

True God—God of Truth

"Show me Your ways, O LORD; teach me Your paths. 5 Lead me in Your truth and teach me, for You are the God of my salvation; on You I wait all the day" (Psalm 25: 4-5 NKJV).

The Hebrew word for truth is "emet" meaning certainty, stability, truth, rightness, trustworthiness. Truth is firm, permanent, reliable and something which is established.

- Ponder these words from verses 4-5:
    - o Show me
    - o Teach me
    - o Lead me
- What does the use of these words say about the writer?
- The first, middle and last letters of the Hebrew alphabet form the word "emet"—truth.
    - o What does this reveal about the God of truth, and truth itself?

Pray the Scripture

Lord, Your Word holds this world together. You are the beginning and end of all things. Show me Your ways; teach me Your paths; lead me in Your truth and teach me. Amen.

Meditation Five

I Am the True Vine—God is Love

"I am the vine, you are the branches. He who abides
in Me, and I in him, bears much fruit; for without Me
you can do nothing. 6 If anyone does not abide in
Me, he is cast out as a branch and is withered; and
they gather them and throw them into the fire, and
they are burned. 7 If you abide in Me, and My words
abide in you, you will ask what you desire, and it shall
be done for you. 8 By this My Father is glorified, that
you bear much fruit; so you will be My disciples. 9 As
the Father loved Me, I also have loved you; abide in
My love. 10 If you keep My commandments, you will
abide in My love, just as I have kept My Father's
commandments and abide in His love" (John 15: 5-10
NKJV).

John 15: 1-17 reflects on Isaiah 5: 1-7 in which Israel is compared to
a vineyard under God's loving care. Identify and write down the
similarities between these two passages of Scripture.

"Now let me sing to my Well-beloved a song of my
Beloved regarding His vineyard: My Well-beloved has
a vineyard on a very fruitful hill. 2 He dug it up and
cleared out its stones, and planted it with the choicest
vine. He built a tower in its midst, and also made a
winepress in it; so He expected it to bring forth good
grapes, but it brought forth wild grapes. 3 "And now,
O inhabitants of Jerusalem and men of Judah, judge,
please, between Me and My vineyard. 4 What more
could have been done to My vineyard that I have not
done in it? Why then, when I expected it to bring

forth good grapes, did it bring forth wild grapes? 5 And now, please let Me tell you what I will do to My vineyard: I will take away its hedge, and it shall be burned; and break down its wall, and it shall be trampled down. 6 I will lay it waste; it shall not be pruned or dug, but there shall come up briers and thorns. I will also command the clouds that they rain no rain on it." 7 For the vineyard of the LORD of hosts is the house of Israel, and the men of Judah are His pleasant plant. He looked for justice, but behold oppression; for righteousness, but behold a cry for help" (Isaiah 5: 1-7 NKJV).

- What do these verses in John 15 and Isaiah 5 reveal about God?
- What does God expect to find in His vineyard?
- What is the consequence of fruitlessness?
- What is the outcome of abiding in Christ? (John 15: 7-11)
- How does Jesus define discipleship in verse 8?
- What does it mean to abide in Him?

Pray the Scripture

Lord, cleanse, purge, trim and remove the excesses in my life, so that I may become fruitful in the kingdom of God. I want to display Your glory. Amen.

Meditation Six

God is Our Father

"In this manner, therefore, pray: Our Father in heaven, hallowed be Your name. 10 Your kingdom come. Your will be done on earth as it is in heaven. 11 Give us this day our daily bread. 12 And forgive us our debts, as we forgive our debtors. 13 And do not lead us into temptation, but deliver us from the evil one. For Yours is the kingdom and the power and the glory forever. Amen 14 "For if you forgive men their trespasses, your heavenly Father will also forgive you. 15 But if you do not forgive men their trespasses, neither will your Father forgive your trespasses" (Matthew 6: 9-15 NKJV).

- What are the major topics of the Lord's Prayer? List them.
- Which human needs are represented, e.g. the need for a father?
- This prayer is addressed to "Our Father".
    - What does this teach about our shared life in the Body of Christ, and in particular about corporate prayer?
- Identify the factors that connect heaven and earth.
- This prayer implies our total dependence upon God.

Pray the Scripture

O God, You are our Father, but You are also my Father. I revere Your name in every part of my life. I yield to Your rule and reign in my heart and mind. Thank you for providing all I need and for keeping me from temptation and Satan himself. Yours is the kingdom, the power and the glory forever. Amen.

Meditation Seven

God is Sovereign

"God is our refuge and strength, a very present help in trouble. 2 Therefore we will not fear, even though the earth be removed, and though the mountains be carried into the midst of the sea; 3 though its waters roar and be troubled, though the mountains shake with its swelling. Selah

4 There is a river whose streams shall make glad the city of God, the holy place of the tabernacle of the Most High. 5 God is in the midst of her, she shall not be moved; God shall help her, just at the break of dawn. 6 The nations raged, the kingdoms were moved; He uttered His voice, the earth melted. 7 The LORD of hosts is with us; the God of Jacob is our refuge. Selah

8 Come; behold the works of the LORD, Who has made desolations in the earth. 9 He makes wars cease to the end of the earth; He breaks the bow and cuts the spear in two; He burns the chariot in the fire. 10 Be still, and know that I am God; I will be exalted among the nations, I will be exalted in the earth! 11 The LORD of hosts is with us; the God of Jacob is our refuge" (Psalm 46: 1-11 NKJV).

We often think of verses 10 and 11 as a call to hush or for silent worship. The setting is war, war against wickedness. God says, "Cease, desist from your efforts; no matter how bad it looks, it is I, God, who will be exalted in victory". Wickedness will not triumph; the enemies of God will not triumph.

- What reassurance does this Psalm offer?
- How does this Psalm describe our God?
- Who is our help and who is our shelter?

Pray the Scripture

O God, I wait upon You until I know for sure that You are my strength all day long. Arrange my days that I may be in the right place at the right time for Your sovereign plan and purposes to unfold. I declare that wickedness will not triumph—You triumph in all things. Amen.

THE AUTHORS

Mintie Nel, single, was born in Calvinia, South Africa and Jan Whitmore, a widow (2011), was born in Bath, England.

From 1992 - 2002, as founders and directors of Mission Encouragement Trust, they travelled throughout Eastern Europe in a motor caravan, pastorally visiting missionaries. Many new opportunities for the Gospel had opened up in Poland, Hungary and Romania after "the wall" had come down. Mintie and Jan were on the frontline offering hands-on support, care and encouragement to missionaries from a vast array of mission agencies.

From 2002 - 2014, they changed their method of providing encouragement. Instead of making field visits, they hosted spiritual retreats for missionaries. Focusing on single workers, they hired suitable and well-appointed retreat centres in South Africa, Eastern Europe, UK and the Middle East. Gathering a staff team and seeking God for very specific direction, their Bible teaching inspired many with themes lifting flagging spirits. Over 600 missionaries, representing 26 mission agencies and 66 nations of service, found encouragement and help to continue in mission service. Mintie & Jan urged local church people to partner in this initiative by sponsoring the missionaries to attend.

In 2014, Mission Encouragement Trust closed and Mintie and Jan became ministry associates of Making Disciples International. From their home in the UK, they combine the debriefing and encouragement of missionaries with an itinerant discipleship ministry. Churches, house groups and mission agencies invite them to bring their own brand of gracious, lively and hands-on discipleship teaching and training. They share from a breadth of experience on important discipleship themes using materials they have both written and proven.

BIBLIOGRAPHY

Bevere, John. *Breaking Intimidation*, Charisma House (1995), a part of Strang Communications Company, Lake Mary, FL 32746

Bevere, John. Drawing Near, Thomas Nelson Publishers (2006)

Bilheimer, Paul E. *Don't Waste your Sorrows,* CLC Publications (1977)

Frangipane, Francis. *Holiness, Truth, and the Presence of God,* Potomac, MD: Arrow Publications (1986).

Nee, Watchman. *The Ministry of God's Word*, Christian Fellowship Publishers, Inc (1971).

Piper, John. *Think: The Life of the Mind and the Love of God*, Desiring God Foundation (2010), Crossway, Illinois 60187

Prince, Derek. *God's Medicine Bottle*, Whittaker House (1984), Derek Prince Ministries International, Charlotte, NC 28219

Ross, Yanit. *Fashioned for Glory*, Making Disciples International (2013). www.amazon.com

Thompson, Dr. Bruce and Barbara. *Walls of my Heart,* Crown Ministries International (1989). Euclid, MN 56722

Tverberg, Lois and Spangler, Ann. *Sitting at the feet of Rabbi Jesus* (2009): Zondervan, Grand Rapids, Michigan 49530

Whitmore, Jan. *Sow What?* Westbow Press (2013). www.amazon.com

Wommack, Andrew, Spirit, Soul, Body, Andrew Wommack Ministries Inc. (2010), CO 80907

Contact: UKOfficeMDI@aol.com

Website: www.makingdisciples.co.uk

"All authority has been given to Me in heaven and on earth. Go therefore and make disciples of all the nations, baptising them in the name of the Father and of the Son and of the Holy Spirit, teaching them to observe all things that I have commanded you; and lo, I am with you always, even to the end of the age." Amen (Matthew 28: 18-20 NKJV).

Made in the USA
Charleston, SC
23 November 2015